The Tiger tank is arguably the most famous armoured vehicle of the Second World War period. Produced in relatively small numbers and employed on the Russian Front, in North Africa, in Italy and in the West these large, powerful tanks were both feared and respected by Allied tank crews who were certain that every German anti-tank gun they encountered was an 88 and every tank was a Tiger.

The development of a heavy breakthrough tank - or *Durchbruchswagen* - began as early as 1937 when the firm of Henschel und Sohn of Kassel was asked to design a tank in the 30 to 33 ton class that would eventually replace the Pzkw IV medium tank which was just then entering service. Through the last months of peace and into 1940 Henschel worked on a number of new designs and Daimler-Benz, Porsche and MAN also received contracts to develop experimental vehicles.

The real impetus came, however, with the invasion of the Soviet Union in 1941 and the Wehrmacht's first confrontation with the Russian T-34. The shock of encountering an enemy tank which combined thick, sloped armour with mobility and firepower cannot be underestimated and to a large extent coloured the thinking of the German military planners and tank designers for the remainder of the war.

Although the development of the 30 ton tanks was to continue Hitler demanded that work begin immediately on a still heavier vehicle with armour that would withstand any anti-tank gun then in use and with capability to destroy any enemy tank at ranges of 1,500 metres. In addition to this the vehicle was to have design would firing a tungsten core projectile, an innovation for its day and a weapon which would have adequately fulfilled expectations. However, the supply of tungsten could not be guaranteed and the only other comparable weapon was the 8.8cm KwK36 which was based on the Flak 18 anti-aircraft gun that had also proven itself in the anti-tank role.

Working day and night the Henschel designers and engineers completed a prototype in under a year loading it onto the railway car which was to transport the tank to Hitler's headquarters at Rastenburg in East Prussia just 40 minutes before the train was scheduled to leave.

The prototype developed by Porsche was sent at the same time and on 19 April 1942 both arrived at the rail junction near Rastenburg. As it was offloaded by a crane the Porsche tank immediately sank into the soft ground and could not extricate itself. Dr Ferdinand Porsche, who accompanied his prototype, is supposed to have curtly refused the offer of Henschel's chief designer to tow his tank free. In the event both tanks crawled the final 11 kilometres to Rastenburg, breaking down continuously and having to be nursed through the entire length of the journey.

On the following day both prototype tanks were presented to Hitler and put through their paces. In many respects the Porsche vehicle proved the be the most impressive, however, both Hitler and Speer, his armaments minister, were swayed by the superior manoeuvrability displayed by the Henschel prototype, just as its designers knew they

A mid production Tiger I of 3.Kompanie, schwere Panzer-Abteilung 502 photographed near Daugavpils, formerly Dünaburg, in Latvia during the late summer of 1944. Note the field modified bracket holding the spare track links on the hull front to the right of the driver's visor. Other photographs from this series show that this is Tiger number 308 and the number is partly visible just behind the driver's head.

SCHWERE PANZER-ABTEILUNG JUNE 1944

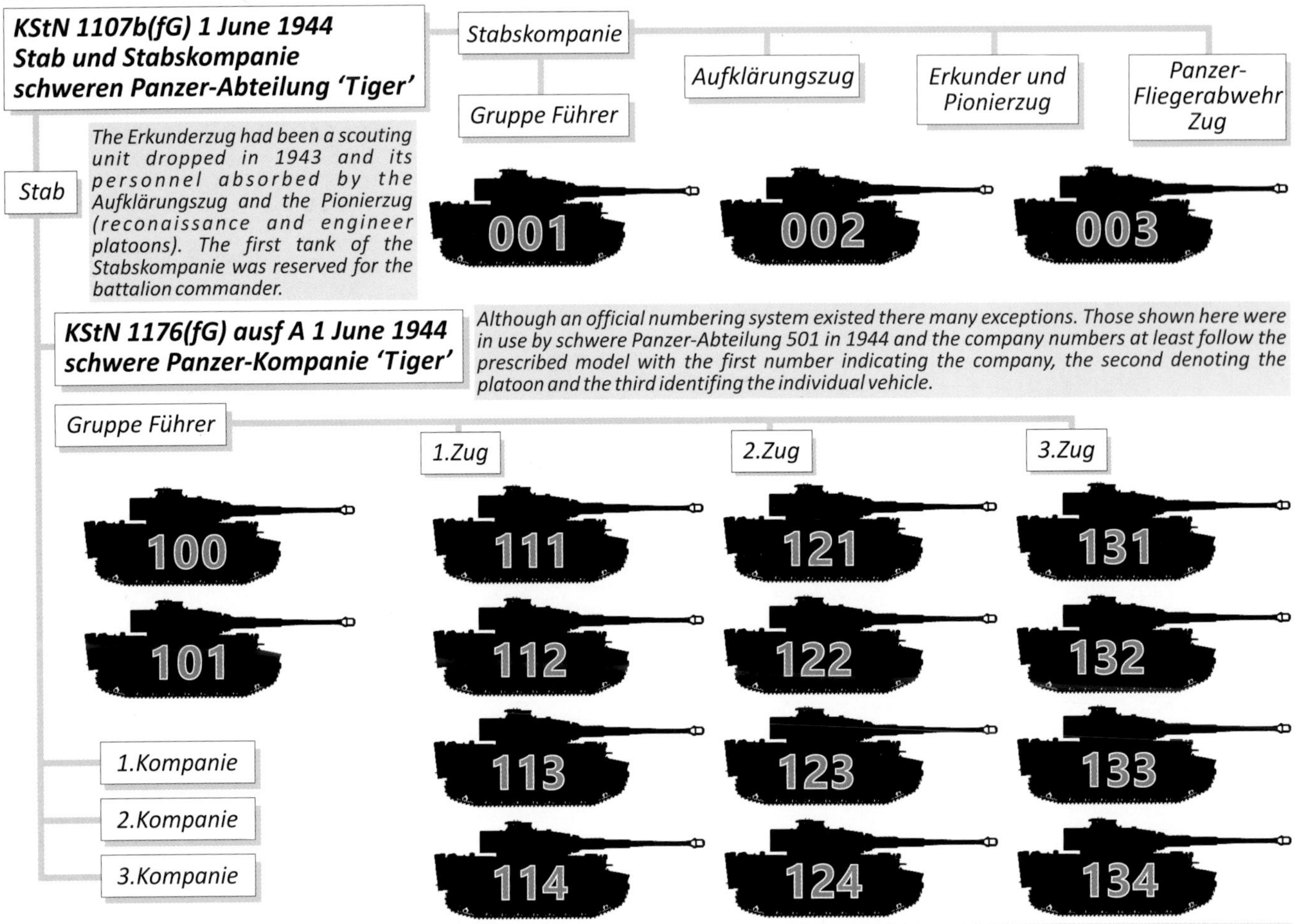

**KStN 1107b(fG) 1 June 1944
Stab und Stabskompanie
schweren Panzer-Abteilung 'Tiger'**

Stabskompanie

Gruppe Führer

Aufklärungzug

Erkunder und Pionierzug

Panzer-Fliegerabwehr Zug

Stab

The Erkunderzug had been a scouting unit dropped in 1943 and its personnel absorbed by the Aufklärungzug and the Pionierzug (reconaissance and engineer platoons). The first tank of the Stabskompanie was reserved for the battalion commander.

001 002 003

**KStN 1176(fG) ausf A 1 June 1944
schwere Panzer-Kompanie 'Tiger'**

Although an official numbering system existed there many exceptions. Those shown here were in use by schwere Panzer-Abteilung 501 in 1944 and the company numbers at least follow the prescribed model with the first number indicating the company, the second denoting the platoon and the third identifying the individual vehicle.

Gruppe Führer

1.Zug 2.Zug 3.Zug

100 111 121 131
101 112 122 132

1.Kompanie 113 123 133
2.Kompanie
3.Kompanie 114 124 134

All units of the German Army were organised according to general orders issued by Oberkommando des Heeres - the high command of the Army - referred to as Heeresmittleitung. When organisational changes were called for these orders were accompanied by Kriegstärkenachweisung - usually abbreviated to KStN - which were detailed tables of establishment showing the official composition of a unit in detail, listing the exact number of personnel and type of equipment from small arms to vehicles. The battalion shown here reflects those issued for 1 June 1944.

would be and it was ordered into production as Panzerkampfwagen VI H (8.8cm) SdKfz 182 ausführung H1 (1).

Although talks had been held regarding the eventual replacement for the Tiger I before production had even begun, it was not until January 1943 that an order was placed for a new heavy tank mounting an even more powerful gun. Again Henschel and Porsche were contracted to develop prototypes and the details of this are discussed in the section on technical details and production modifications for the Tiger II beginning on page 61.

As mentioned earlier, the Tiger was envisaged as a breakthrough weapon and it was originally intended that company sized units of twenty vehicles would be attached to Panzer divisions and employed as spearhead formations. These companies would be made up of Tigers and light tanks which were capable of performing duties for which the Tigers were unsuitable. Indeed many field commanders considered it a mistake when the light tanks were eventually dropped from the battalion table of organisation. The first battalions, formed in 1942, were made up of Pzkw III ausf J and Pzkw III ausf N tanks, the latter armed with a 7.5cm gun, and twenty Tigers. By the end of 1942, after some initial confusion, each battalion was organised with a Stabskompanie, or headquarters company, with two

Tigers and one Pzkw III, with an attached light company of five Pzkw III tanks. The battalion's two tank companies were each controlled by a headquarters troop of a single Tiger and two Pzkw III tanks and contained four platoons of two Tigers and two Pzkw III.

On 5 March 1943 a complete reorganisation saw the light tanks removed and the companies reduced to three platoons of four Tigers each. The number of companies in a battalion was however increased to three meaning that a complete schwere Panzer-Abteilung could field forty-five tanks. Beginning in early 1944 a system referred to in German as *Freie Gliederung*, which translates roughly as free organisation, was gradually introduced throughout the army. In practice this meant that transport elements were removed from company commands and concentrated at battalion or regimental level.

On 1 June 1944 new organisational instructions were issued for Tiger battalions which reflected the *Freie Gliederung* principles but these had no effect on the number of tanks although they did allow for either the Tiger I or Tiger II and separate instructions were issued for companies equipped with radio-controlled demolition vehicles. On 1 November new orders were issued for the organisation of the Tiger battalions but these were little more than name changes.

1)This name was in use until 5 March 1943 when the more familiar title Panzerkampfwagen Tiger (8.8cm L/56) SdKfz 181 ausführung E came into use.

CENTRAL AND EASTERN EUROPE 1940 - 1945

National borders and frontiers are shown as they were in 1944.

In January 1944 the front line ran from Lake Ladoga east of Leningrad - which had been surrounded since 1941 - down to Novgorod then on to Polotsk, east of Vitebsk and Orscha, south through the Pripet marshes to the west of Kiev and from there followed the Dnieper to the Black Sea. On the eve of Operation Bagration in June 1944, the line had changed little in the north but in the centre had bulged towards Kovel and Tarnopol and in the south from near Balti followed the line of the Dniester to the coast. By mid-August the Russians had advanced to the Vistula in the centre and had overrun approximately half of both Latvia and Lithuania in the north. On the last day of 1944 the Red Army occupied all of the Baltic States, except the Kurland region of northern Latvia, most of Poland and in the south had crossed the Danube. In addition both Romania and Bulgaria had surrendered. During the war many towns and villages of Czechoslovakia, Poland, Belarus and Ukraine were forced to revert to the German names that had been in use up to 1918, prior to which they had either been part of the German Empire or originally founded by German settlers. With very few exceptions these names were abolished after 1945 as were the names of the towns and cities of East Prussia and Silesia which were given Russian or Polish names. With the fall of the Soviet Union in the 1990s the majority of locations in the new eastern republics were given new names, often bearing little or no resemblance to their former title. In view of this I have endeavoured to use the names that readers will be most familiar with which may be a mixture of former and current.

The development of a heavy, breakthrough tank - or *Durchbruchwagen* - had begun as early as 1937 and after extensive discussion it was envisaged that they should be employed in small, independent formations controlled by Corps or Army level commands and attached to divisions. The first units formed were two companies, both created on 16 February 1942, as schwere Panzer-Kompanie 501 and schwere Panzer-Kompanie 502. The exact make up of these companies is not clear as detailed organisational charts were not issued until 25 April 1942 when the first battalion-sized unit was created. These charts and tables - or Kriegsstärkenachweisungen, usually abbreviated to KStN - regulated the composition of every unit of the German Army and are discussed on page 2. By the end of the war eleven heavy battalions had been created for the Army and three for the Waffen-SS, together with the heavy company that remained with SS-Panzer-Regiment 3 until May 1945. Other units were equipped with Tiger tanks, most importantly the formations which controlled the Sprengstoffträger radio-controlled explosive charge carriers, but these for the most part operated in the west and so are not included here. Following are brief histories of the heavy tank units and although some details pre-date our study they are included to give the reader a more complete picture of the development and history of the heavy tank formations.

SCHWERE PANZER-ABTEILUNG 501

The army's first heavy tank battalion was formed on 10 May 1942 from schwere Panzer-Kompanien 501 and 502, which were later renamed as the battalion's first and second companies. Further personnel were drawn from Panzer-Ersatz-Abteilung 1, a replacement and training unit stationed at Erfurt in Germany and from Panzerschiess-Schule Putlos, a tank gunnery school near Holstein.

It was originally intended that this battalion would be equipped with the Tiger (P) which was then being developed by Porsche and a number of drivers were sent to the Nibelungenwerke at St.Valentin in Austria to be trained on the new tanks. The decision to drop the Porsche design in favour of Henschel's proposal in July delayed the battalion's training and formation and the first two Tigers did not arrive until 30 August 1942. The battalion's first and second companies were sent to North Africa, the latter via France, with the first tanks arriving on 23 November 1942. So precarious was the supply route from Italy to the African coast that the last Tigers did not reach Tunisia until late January 1943 and the battalion's 3.Kompanie, which was not fully formed until 6 March, remained in Europe and was eventually attached to Panzer-Regiment Grossdeutschland as a

tenth company. On 12 May 1943 the remnants of the battalion, which had been combined with elements of the newly arrived schwere Panzer-Abteilung 504, surrendered to the British near El Alia in Tunisia. Beginning on 9 September 1943, and employing some 150 veterans of the original formation, the battalion was rebuilt under the command of Major Erich Löwe, an experienced tank officer who had been awarded the Knight's Cross as a company commander during the 1940 French Campaign. The battalion spent the following months in training and on Sunday, 5 December 1943 began moving to the Eastern Front. From 19 December until the end of the year the battalion was involved in the fierce fighting between Losovka and Vitebsk and it was here, on 23 December, that the battalion commander was killed.

In January and February 1944 the battalion was operating in the area around Vitebsk, north-east of Minsk in modern day Belarus, in support of Panzergrenadier-Division Feldherrnhalle and 14.Infanterie-Division. Despite the heavy fighting just one Tiger was lost at this time when an artillery shell landed directly on the turret roof of Leutnant Schröder's tank. In early March 1944, with just seventeen serviceable tanks, the battalion took part in

Mid production Tigers of 2.Kompanie, schwere Panzer-Abteilung 501 said to have been photographed during Operation Hubertus in early March 1944. The accompanying grenadiers are probably from 256.Infanterie-Division.

Both tanks have the cast commander's cupola introduced in July 1943, although they appear to retain the mountings for the two front headlights which were dropped at about the same time. The loader's hatch of the tank nearest the camera has the small outside lock adjuster fitted to its centre that was deleted from production in September 1943. The turret ventilation fan - the flat, raised disc in front of the cupola - was moved from the rear of the turret roof to the position seen here in July 1943.

Tiger II tanks of 3.Kompanie, schwere Panzer-Abteilung 501 photographed in late 1944. The vehicle furthest from the camera appears to be painted in a Dunkelgelb base coat only without any disruptive camouflage. The tank in the foreground, Tiger 313, is also shown in the illustration section on page 19.

EQUIPMENT ALLOCATIONS AND LOSSES, SCHWERE PANZER-ABTEILUNG 501, 1944

		Jan	Feb	Mar	Apr	May	Jun	Jul	Aug	Sep	Oct	Nov	Dec
s.Pz-Abt 501	*Received*						6	At this time the battalion began leaving the East for					
Tiger I	*Lost*	1	9				23*	Germany to re-equip with the Tiger II. The last 2					
	On Hand	38/19	29/17	29/27	29/29	29/29	6 (T)	Tiger I tanks were lost on 5 July 1944.					
	*9 tanks to sPz-Abt 509. Figures shown in On Hand column are total followed by combat ready; (T) Total available												
s.Pz-Abt 501	*Received*	In addition to the allocation of Tiger II, an					6	27*	12	14***			
Tiger II	*Lost*	unknown number of Tiger I tanks were							4				
	On Hand	taken over from sPz-Abt 509 in September					6 (T)	33 (T)	41/26**	53/36	49 (O)	51 (O)	
	* 2 from sPz-Abt 505; **Last delivery 7 August; *** From sPz-Abt 509. (O) Operational; (T) Total												

Operation Hubertus, a limited offensive to retake the village of Osipenki west of Vitebsk near the current Belarus frontier, with the assault guns of Sturmgeschütz-Brigade 281 and the grenadiers of 256.Infanterie-Division. In early June nine Tigers were handed over to schwere Panzer-Abteilung 509 leaving just twenty tanks in total. On 23 June 1944, the day after the commencement of the Soviet Operation Bagration, the battalion was rushed to the area north-east of Orscha, an important rail and road junction on the Dnieper river, and immediately faced strong Russian armoured units including a number of JS-2 heavy tanks. The fighting here was extremely confused and the tanks of the battalion were widely dispersed. During the withdrawal across the Dnieper the tank of the first platoon commander crashed through the bridge and could not be recovered. In addition several other tanks were abandoned due to lack of fuel. The battalion continued to withdraw to the west and on 2 July 1944 the six remaining operational Tigers were ferried across the Berezina river.

Over the next few days a number of tanks were delivered from depot workshops and thrown into the defence of Minsk but most were abandoned after they ran out of fuel and two simply went missing and were never seen again. All surviving crews were withdrawn to Germany where, on 17 July 1944, the battalion was reformed. Equipped with a full complement of tanks the second and third companies returned to the front and on 11 August and were attached to 16.Panzer-Division and immediately thrown into an attack between Chmielnik and Szydlow in central Poland in an effort to reduce the so called Sandomierz Bulge. At the same time, 1.Kompanie was leaving Ohrdruf in Germany and within a week, in a dramatic turn of events, the battalion commander, Oberstleutnant von Legat, was removed from his post over suspicions of his involvement in the July plot to assassinate Hitler (1). In September the battalion was attached to XXXVIII.Panzerkorps and took part in the defensive battles near Kielce and Ostrowiec on the western bank of the Vistula. At this time a number of Tiger I tanks were handed over from schwere Panzer-Abteilung 509, which was returning to Germany (2), and by the end of September the battalion reported that fifty-three tanks in total were on hand, with thirty-six of those being combat ready. On 1 December 1944 the battalion was able to field fifty-one operational Tigers and on 21 December was renamed schwere Panzer-Abteilung 424 to avoid confusion with schwere SS-Panzer-Abteilung 501. On the last day of 1944 the battalion reported that seventeen Tigers were fully operational.

1.The eventual fate of von Legat is not known, however, his name does not appear of the list of those charged and tried and he may have been exonerated. He was replaced by Major Saemisch who was killed while leading the battalion at Lisow in January 1945.
2.The exact number of Tiger I tanks is not known but schwere Panzer-Abteilung 501 reported forty-two tanks in total on 12 August 1944 and the subsequent loss of one tank by September indicating that schwere Panzer-Abteilung 509 may have relinquished as many as twelve Tigers from its total of thirteen tanks.

SCHWERE PANZER-ABTEILUNG 502

Formed on 25 May 1942 from Panzer-Ersatz-Abteilung 35, this unit was not the first of the heavy tank battalions created by the German Army, as is sometimes stated, although it was the first to receive an allocation of Tigers and the first to see action, 1.Kompanie going into combat on 21 September 1942 near Tortolovo, some 30 kilometres east of Leningrad on the Volkov Front.

These first tanks suffered almost continuous mechanical failures and during the training phase were only kept operational with the help of civilian maintenance crews from the Henschel factory temporarily attached to the battalion.

On 29 August 1942, of the four Tigers available to 1.Kompanie, off loaded at the railway junction at Mga near Leningrad, three broke down before they could reach their assigned position at the front. Although the fourth made contact with the enemy it became bogged and had to be towed to safety.

The battalion's 2.Kompanie was formed from surplus crews of Panzer-Regiment 1 and Panzer-Regiment 35 and arrived in Russia on 7 January 1943 to be attached to Heeresgruppe Don operating in the southern Ukraine, far from the battalion's headquarters and first company fighting on the Volkov. It seems the lessons of 1942 had been learnt, however, as the company was able to make the road march from Proletarsk, south-east of Rostov, to Ssungar (1), a journey of over 100 kilometres, on their own tracks without a single mechanical failure.

On 22 February 1943 the battalion's second company was transferred to schwere Panzer-Abteilung 503 and renamed as that formation's third company. While 1.Kompanie remained in the east, a new 2.Kompanie was formed in France from men of Panzer-Regiment 3 and by the end of May a third company had been raised, mainly from personnel of Panzer-Regiment 4.

By the end of July the new companies, together with the battalion staff, were reunited with 1.Kompanie in time to take part in the battles to the south of Leningrad, now Saint Petersburg.

During the remainder of the year the battalion fought in the attempts to retake Newel, south of Pskov, and as the new year approached, 1.Kompanie was transferred to the Leningrad sector.

In January 1944 the remainder of the battalion, which was still with VIII.Armeekorps near Newel was rushed to Gatshina, south of Leningrad , in an effort to halt the Soviet attempts to break out of the Oranienbaum bridgehead. The third company commanded by Leutnant Meyer formed a Kampfgruppe with 9.Luftwaffen-Feld-Division and Grenadier-Regiment 422 and when the first and second companies arrived they were formed into a battle group with Grenadier-Regiment 377 and Panzerjäger-Kompanie 240 (2).

In the confused and desperate fighting that took place around Syaskelevo eleven Tigers were completely destroyed while a number had to be towed during the withdrawal to Volosovo. The commander of 3.Kompanie, Leutnant Meyer, finding himself surrounded, committed suicide rather than surrender and Oberleutnant Diesl, the commander of 1.Kompanie, was killed near Narva on the last day of the month.

A mid production Tiger I of schwere Panzer-Abteilung 502. This tank is shown and discussed further in the illustration section on page 20. I am indebted to Hartmut von Holdt who was able to identify this vehicle as Tiger number 305 of the battalion's 3.Kompanie.

1.The location is given by both Schneider and Carius. I have been unable to locate Ssungar on any modern map but as Schneider's account states 2.Kompanie was in action at Ozerskiy by the next day and Bratskiy on the following day, Ssungar may be modern Yuzhnyy which sits astride the road network west of Bratskiy.
2.This is almost certainly a company of Panzerjäger-Abteilung 240 from 170.Infanterie-Division.

A mid production Tiger I of 2.Kompanie, schwere Panzer-Abteilung 502. The use of a white outline and the placement of the company number were both identifying features of this battalion's tanks.

In early February the battalion was moved to Narva-Joesuu on the Gulf of Finland north of Narva, and remained in the area until mid-April, taking part in the attempts to reduce the Soviet bridgeheads on the western bank of the Narva river near Auvere and east of modern Sirgala (1) referred to by the Germans as the Ostsack and Westsack respectively.

During this time the companies were separated and fought with the units that were collectively known as Panzer-Kampfgruppe Strachwitz (2). Operations in the Narva area only ceased when the ground, already marshy, became impassable in mid-April and the battalion used the next seven weeks to carry out urgently needed repairs.

When the Soviet summer offensive began on 22 June the battalion was attached to XXXVII.Armeekorps in the Pskov-Ostrov area, near the junction of the present day Estonian, Latvian and Russian borders. The second and third companies were ordered to counterattack immediately towards the Velikaya river in support of 121.Infanterie-Division while 1.Kompanie was temporarily attached to the neighbouring I.Armeekorps. The Tigers were employed for the most part in platoon-sized groups in support of infantry and combat engineer units and during this time had their first experience of the US M4 Sherman tank when a single example was destroyed by Leutnant Eichorn of 2.Kompanie. On Sunday, 2 July

the battalion began moving to Dünaburg, modern Daugavpils in Latvia, the last tanks arriving on the following Thursday. At that time the battalion was able to report that twenty-two Tigers were combat ready from a total of fifty-two. Four tanks had been abandoned in the battles near Ostrov and had to be destroyed by German artillery.

During July and most of August small units of the battalion - sometimes individual tanks - fought along the Duna river in an effort to hold back the Red Army. It was here on 22 July that 2.Kompanie under Leutnant Otto Carius with just eight Tigers ambushed and destroyed twenty-eight Russian tanks in a single action near Krivani, 12 kilometres north of Daugavpils off the road to Kalupe.

Despite local successes the battalion had lost twenty-seven tanks by late August, at least four of those to captured 88mm guns, and the heavier and more powerful armoured vehicles including the JS-2 tank and ISU-152 self propelled gun which the Russians were by now employing.

On 25 August the battalion moved to Ergli, coming under the command of X.Armeekorps of Heeresgruppe Nord, and fought here in the defence of the port city of Riga claiming, on 26 September, to have destroyed its 1000th Soviet tank since the battalion arrived in Russia almost exactly two years previously.

1. Both Schneider and Carius refer to a village in this area named Krissavo. Since 1955 a system of large reservoirs have been constructed to the south of the city of Narva and many of the small villages and hamlets mentioned in 1944 no longer exist.
2. Commanded by Oberst Graf Strachwitz von Gross-Zauche und Camminetz, the establishment of this ad-hoc unit changed several times and also included elements of the Fuhrer-Begleit-Bataillon and Panzergrenadier-Division Feldherrnhalle. In his account of the battles Otto Carius, who was present, also mentions a number of Pzkw IV tanks and Nebelwerfers from Panzergrenadier-Division Grossdeutschland as well as infantry and halftracks of the division's fusilier regiment. Sources differ over the exact name of Strachwitz's command and I have chosen to use the version which was used with the award of the Diamonds to his Knight's Cross.

EQUIPMENT ALLOCATIONS AND LOSSES, SCHWERE PANZER-ABTEILUNG 502, 1944

		Jan	Feb	Mar	Apr	May	Jun	Jul	Aug	Sep	Oct	Nov	Dec
s.Pz-Abt 502	*Received*	22	30										2*
	Lost	17			4	4	9	17	10	6		7**	
	On Hand	41 (T)	71 (T)		67/25	63/22	54 (T)	37 (T)	27 (T)	21 (T)	16 (O)	14 (T)	16 (T)
	* From PzRgt GD; ** 6 to sPz-Abt 510;												

On 4 October the battalion was ordered to begin preparations to move to Germany to re-train on the Tiger II, however, five days later Red Army units reached the Baltic coast near Memel, modern Klaipeda in Lithuania, cutting off the units of Heeresgruppe Nord and all transport was halted.

Over the next days Hauptmann Leonhardt's 3.Kompanie with its remaining eight Tigers was attached to schwere Panzer-Abteilung 510 while the thirteen tanks of the first and second companies were employed in the defence of the Memel bridgehead.

On 30 October the crews without tanks, who had been fighting as infantry, were withdrawn to Gdansk and on 12 November Leutnant Leonhardt's men, after handing over their last six tanks to schwere Panzer-Abteilung 510, were evacuated to Libau, present day Liepaja in Latvia, and from there to Gdansk and finally Paderborn in Germany.

The first and second companies would remain in Memel until 21 January 1945 when they were withdrawn to Germany, managing to take with them the last three surviving Tigers.

SCHWERE PANZER-ABTEILUNG 503

Formed with two companies on 16 April 1942 from tank crews of Panzer-Regiment 5 and Panzer-Regiment 6, this battalion, like schwere Panzer-Abteilung 501, had trained briefly on the Porsche Tiger before the decision was made to manufacture the Henschel version. Originally intended for service in North Africa, the first allocation of tanks were modified for service in a tropical climate - presumably the twenty Tigers and Pzkw III ausf N tanks recorded as converted for operations in Russia from 16 December 1942. The battalion was sent to the Eastern Front in January 1943 and took part in the defensive battles following the retreat from the Caucasus.

On 22 January the second company of schwere Panzer-Abteilung 502, which had been attached and operating under the battalion's command for some time, was formally transferred and became 3.Kompanie, schwere Panzer-Abteilung 503. During July the battalion took part in Operation Citadel with the first, second and third companies attached to 6.Panzer-Division, 19.Panzer-Division and 7.Panzer-Division respectively. In August the battalion operated with the Waffen-SS divisions Das Reich, Totenkopf and Wiking in what is today eastern Ukraine and by the end of September all thirty-nine Tigers were with repair workshops.

By the end of the year the remnants of the battalion, with just four combat ready tanks, was located between Zhmerynka and Khmelnytskyi. In January 1944 the battalion was attached to schwere Panzer-Regiment Bäke (1) and took part in the counterattacks east of Vinnitsa in central Ukraine and fought in the battles to relieve the German forces trapped in the Tscherkassy pocket.

Below left: The battalion commander's Tiger I photographed in January 1944. Note the Zimmerit coating and the spare tracks on the turret side. The tank's identifying number, a Roman I, can just be seen on the turret side in front of the vision port. The officer standing in the cupola is almost certainly Hauptmann Clemens-Heinrich Graf von Kageneck who left the battalion at the end of January after being wounded. At right is a mid production Tiger I of 3.Kompanie. The application of the two Balkankreuz markings on either side of the company number was common to the tanks of this battalion in late 1943 and early 1944.

1.Commanded by Oberstleutnant Dr. Franz Bäke, this ad-hoc formation included the battalion's thirty-four Tigers, the headquarters staff from Panzer-Regiment 11 and the second battalion of Panzer-Regiment 23 equipped with forty-seven Panther tanks. In addition, Bäke's unit was supported by a number of self-propelled guns from Artillerie-Regiment 88 together with infantry from 4.Gebirgs-Division and an engineer battalion. This formation was disbanded in late January 1944 and should not be confused with gepanzerte Gruppe Bäke which was formed in the following March.

On 17 February, when the units in Tscherkassy began the breakout, the battalion had been reduced to just eight serviceable tanks. On 1 March 1944 the battalion was attached to 4.Panzerarmee near Proskurov, today Khmelnytskyi in Western Ukraine, and within days - with thirteen combat ready Tigers - was again in action in support of Panzer-Regiment 25 in defensive operations around Ternopil and eventually the attempts to break out of the Kamenets-Podolski pocket in western Ukraine. By 22 April schwere Panzer-Abteilung 503 had lost all but seven of its tanks including twenty-one vehicles captured when the battalion's maintenance facilities were overrun. In May the battalion was ordered to Germany to be re-equipped with the Tiger II, the surviving tanks handed over to schwere Panzer-Abteilung 509.

Earlier, in January 1944, a small detachment under Leutnant Günter Piepgras of 1.Kompanie had been sent to Germany to pick up twelve Tigers which had been promised to the battalion. Returning in late February, Piepgras's men were unable to rejoin the battalion and were attached to Kampfgruppe Mittermeier until 16 April when the battle group was disbanded. In early May 1944 the remaining seven tanks, manned by crews of 3.Kompanie, were transferred to 1.Panzerlehrgruppe Nordukraine and tasked with the training of Hungarian army tank crews on the Tiger I. Four of these tanks were eventually transferred to schwere Panzer-Abteilung 509 while one remained with 1.Panzerlehrgruppe Nordukraine.

The battalion was fully refitted with Tiger II tanks and fought in the west until 12 October 1944 when it was rebuilt, after losing most of its tanks in Normandy, and sent to Budapest in Hungary (1). By 18 October the battalion was fighting at the Tisza bridgehead with Panzer-Regiment 24 and later in the counterattacks around Turkeve and Szaparfalu, some 70 kilometres south-east of Budapest, under the command of 4.SS-Polizei-Panzergrenadier-Division. On 1 November the battalion took part in the attack on Kecskemet on the Budapest- Szeged road where 24.Panzer-Division had been encircled. Although the fighting had been heavy and almost continuous, up to this time just one tank had been lost. On 5 November the battalion was moved to the north-east of Budapest and divided into three Kampfgruppen and used as an emergency reserve. At the end of the month the battalion was reunited and moved to Hogyesz, south of Lake Balaton, with fifteen operational Tigers and in mid-December took part in the battles for Stuhlweissenburg, present day Szekesfehervar. By the end of December schwere Panzer-Abteilung 503 was supporting Reiter-Regiment von Mackensen near Pusztavam on the Szekesfehervar - Gyor road with just four operational tanks. During the last eight weeks of 1944 the battalion had lost twenty tanks - half of those in a single day on 7 December when the maintenance facilities at Kurt had been lost to the Russians after a fierce defence conducted for the most part by damaged tanks. In the first week of January the battalion was renamed schwere Panzer-Abteilung Feldherrnhalle.

EQUIPMENT ALLOCATIONS AND LOSSES, SCHWERE PANZER-ABTEILUNG 503, 1944

		Jan	Feb	Mar	Apr	May	Jun	Jul	Aug	Sep	Oct	Nov	Dec
s.Pz-Abt 503	**Received**	43	16*	6			*On 25 May the battalion was withdrawn to Germany to*						
Tiger I	**Lost**	4	18	34	9	20**	*convert to the Tiger II. The battalion was equipped with 45*						
	On Hand	66/13	64/24	36/13	27/7	7***	*new tanks all of which had been lost by August*						
	* 7 from sPz-Abt 506; ** 5 to sPz-Abt 505; *** Handed over to sPz-Abt 509 in late May												
s.Pz-Abt 503	**Received**									45			
Tiger II	**Lost**											7	14
	On Hand									47/47*	47/18	40/11	26/19
	*At least two of these tanks were survivors of the fighting on the Western Front, fitted with the earlier Porsche turret												

A Tiger II of 2.Kompanie, schwere Panzer-Abteilung 503 photographed in Budapest in October 1944. Tanks of this company are also shown and discussed in the illustration section on page 26.

1.Two Tigers with the Porsche turret survived the fighting on the Western Front and were with the battalion in Hungary, at least one with 3.Kompanie.

SCHWERE PANZER-ABTEILUNG 505

Formed on 29 January 1943 with two companies and made up from personnel of 3.Panzer-Division and 26.Panzer-Division, this battalion was originally intended for service in North Africa, but within less than a month the orders had been changed to organise the battalion for deployment in the East. On 3 April, while the battalion was training in Belgium, a third company was created using men from 2.Panzer-Division. The first and second companies of the battalion arrived in Russia by 6 May 1943 but it was 8 July before 3.Kompanie was able to join them by which time the battalion had been engaged in the fighting between Soborovka and Olkhovatka, south of Orel as part of Operational Citadel, for three days.

During the remainder of 1943 the battalion was engaged in defensive fighting around Smolensk and by the end of the year was in the Vitebsk area.

EQUIPMENT ALLOCATIONS AND LOSSES, SCHWERE PANZER-ABTEILUNG 505, 1944

		Jan	Feb	Mar	Apr	May	Jun	Jul	Aug	Sep	Oct	Nov	Dec
s.Pz-Abt 505	Received				23		10*		by 25 July the battalion was withdrawn to				
Tiger I	Lost	5	2				9	12	Germany with 11 Tigers which were handed				
	On Hand	20/17	18/15	18/14	41/18	41/36	42	30**	to the maintenance section at Ohrdruf				
		*Including 9 repaired Tigers; What became of these tanks is unclear with just 11 leaving the front with the battalion											
s.Pz-Abt 505	Received							6	41				
Tiger II	Lost							2*		1	7		
	On Hand							4	45	44/44	37/18	37/30	37/34
	*Handed over to sPz-Abt 501												

An early production Tiger I of 2.Kompanie, schwere Panzer-Abteilung 506 photographed in early 1944. This tank is also shown and discussed on page 24 of the illustration secion.

In January 1944 the battalion took part in the defensive battles between Vitebsk and Polotsk in Belarus supporting 6.Luftwaffen-Feld-Division and then 12.Panzergrenadier-Division. At the end of the month 3.Kompanie, which had been reduced to two tanks, was withdrawn from the front to be rested and re-equipped, and the surviving Tigers were formed into a Kampfgruppe under the command of Oberleutnant Wilhelm Knauth. During February the tanks of the battalion undertook a number of counterattacks as far east as the twin villages of Kovalki and Polyachki, almost exactly halfway between Vitebsk and Smolensk. In March the battalion was operating in the area south-east of Lake Hrodna and Orscha, sixty kilometres south of Vitebsk near the present day Belarus-Russian frontier and during the first weeks was attached to 78.Sturm-Division. In late April the battalion headquarters with 2.Kompanie and 3.Kompanie were transported by rail to Maciejowice, on the eastern bank of the Vistula, were six new tanks

Photographed before the battalion left Germany, this Tiger II of 1.Kompanie, schwere Panzer-Abteilung 506 provides a good view of the colourful unit insignia and its application to the turret side. Note that the company number of 112 is repeated on the turret rear access door. The markings of this battalion is also discussed in the illustration section on page 25.

were received. The Tigers of 1.Kompanie which had been operating with 5.Panzer-Division near Kovel did not return until 9 May by which time the battalion had moved to the village of Stawki, south of Torun, west of the Vistula. A planned counterattack from Myrovychi across the Turiya river was cancelled and most of May and June were spent carrying out badly needed repairs.

In late June the battalion formed part of Gruppe General von Altrock (1) with 5.Panzer-Division fighting to defend Borisov, now Barysaw, in the Minsk region. During the following days schwere Panzer-Abteilung 505 attempted to hold up the Soviet advance east of Minsk towards Barysaw along the Moscow highway in an effort to keep the railway lines open as long as possible while the city was being evacuated. Falling back towards the crossing of the Berezina river, some 40 kilometres east of Minsk, the Tigers were the last to cross as it was feared the wooden bridge would not hold their weight. On 8 July the remaining tanks reached Augustowo, thirty kilometres south of Bialystock in Poland, having lost twenty-one Tigers including six damaged vehicles which could not be salvaged.

Over the next few days the tanks were loaded onto railway cars and transported to Ohrdruf in Germany were the last shipment arrived on 25 July. The remaining eleven Tigers that had survived the fighting were handed over to depot maintenance units and on the following day the first new Tiger II tanks were received. The battalion commander, Major Werner Freiherr von Beschwitz, was later awarded the Knight's Cross for the courage and leadership he had displayed in the battles through eastern Poland.

By 10 September schwere Panzer-Abteilung 505 had returned to the front and was subordinated to 2.Armee as an operational reserve at Nasielsk, 20 kilometres north-west of Warsaw. Almost immediately the battalion was attached to 24.Panzer-Division and took part in the counterattacks along the Narev river bridgehead with elements of schwere Panzer-Abteilung 507. From 30 September the battalion was attached to 3.Panzer-Division and took part in Operation Sonnenblume (2) between Nasielsk and Pultusk north of Nowy Dwor Mazowiecki and the confluence of the Narev and Vistula rivers.

By 14 October the battalion had left Poland and been moved to Virbalis in Lithuania supporting 561.Infanterie-Division in defensive positions around Kairiai near Siaulia in an attempt to block the Soviet advance. By 18 October the German units had been pushed back across the East Prussian border first to Haldenau - which no longer exists - and then to Schleuwen, modern day Chernyshevskoye, where they at least managed to cut off and destroy small local enemy penetrations. In the next few days the battalion was attached to Fallschirm-Panzer-Korps Hermann Göring for a planned attack on Jägershagen near Gumbinnen, modern Grusev. The operation was altered at the last moment and the Tigers advanced towards the south almost reaching Soginten, about 4 kilometres east of the Gumbinnen-Goldap road, before they were threatened with encirclement and withdrew during the night through territory which had been captured by the Russians. The battalion continued to fight in localised defensive battles supporting units of Fallschirm-Panzergrenadier-Division Hermann Göring 2 and parts of the Fuhrer-Begleit-Brigade until 6 November 1944 when the Tigers were withdrawn from the front and relocated to Plauendorf, now Plavni near the present Polish border, as the operational reserve of XXXIX.Panzerkorps.

The battalion spent the remainder of the year repairing and refitting its tanks under a new commander, Major Otto-Friedrich Senfft von Pilsach, who had arrived in November. Incredibly the battalion had lost just four tanks in the fighting through Lithuania and into East Prussia.

1.Within days this large battle group was renamed Gruppe von Gottberg and then Gruppe von Saucken. It was made up primarily from units of 5.Panzer-Division and schwere Panzer-Abteilung 505 with the remnants of XXXIX.Panzerkorps which had been encircled and badly battered in the opening phase of Operation Bagration. The corps had been one of the strongest formations available to Heeresgruppe Mitte in early June but had lost its commander, his replacement and all five division commanders by the end of the month.
2.Confusingly several operations used this codename during the war and this is probably the least documented of all.

SCHWERE PANZER-ABTEILUNG 506

Formed on 20 July 1943 with three companies from men of III.Abteilung, Panzer-Regiment 33 the battalion arrived in Russia in late September of the same year. For much of September and October the companies operated independently attached to various Kampfgruppen fighting in southern Ukraine, west of the Dnieper taking part in the recapture of Krivoy Rog - modern Kryvyi Rih. By the end of the year the battalion had moved further to the west and was attached to III.Panzerkorps operating in the area between Vinnitsa and Uman in support of 16.Panzer-Division and 17.Panzer-Division. The battalion remained in defensive positions between Orativ and Teplyk, about 40 kilometres to the east of Vinnitsa until 20 January when the three operational tanks took part in an assault on Novelskij and Wladisslawtschik (1), north-east of Monastyryshche with the tanks of 16.Panzer-Division. On 25 January the battalion took part in Operation Waldtraut, attacking Russian advance positions near Orativ and Rossoshe north of Vinnitsa losing sixteen tanks in just one week. In early February Schwere Panzer-Abteilung 506, with ten operational tanks, was withdrawn from the front and moved to the area west of Tcherkassy in preparation for an assault to break through to the German troops trapped there. On 1 March the remaining tanks were handed over to schwere Panzer-Abteilung 503 and the crews transferred to Lemberg, now Lviv, where forty-five new Tiger II tanks were delivered between 29 March and 8 April 1944. While deliveries were still underway parts of the battalion were ordered to Pomoryany, on the Berezhany-Zolochiv road, to support 100.Jager-Division in an attack across the Koropietz river towards Beckersdorf, present day Yustynivka. From mid-April the battalion moved to the west bank of the Dnieper near Stanislaw, today Ivano-Frankivsk, and here, through May and much of June, fought as small battle groups often made up of two to three tanks in support of the Panthers of Panzer-Regiment 23. In July the battalion marched over 100 kilometres to Zaliztsi and as part of XIII.Armeekorps fought with 8.Panzer-Division in the unsuccessful counterattacks to relieve Brody some 40 kilometres to the north. In the subsequent withdrawal to Duliby on the Stryi river most of the tanks were abandoned and destroyed by their own crews. On 28 July the battalion handed over the surviving Tigers to schwere panzer-Abteilung 507 and by 15 August the last crews had left for Germany. The battalion was rebuilt and remained in the west until May 1945.

EQUIPMENT ALLOCATIONS AND LOSSES, SCHWERE PANZER-ABTEILUNG 506, 1944

		Jan	Feb	Mar	Apr	May	Jun	Jul	Aug	Sep	Oct	Nov	Dec
s.Pz-Abt 506	*Received*	12	5	24	21				*On 15 August the battalion left for*				
Tiger I	*Lost*	16	3		3	1		7*	*Germany to re-equip with the Tiger II and*				
	On Hand	22/18	24	24/21	42/22	41/39	41/40	34**	*fought in the West until May 1945*				
	** 6 to sPz-Abt 507; ** All lost in combat or destroyed by their own crews*												

A late production Tiger I of 1.Kompanie, schwere Panzer-Abteilung 506. The white number 12 on the turret side identifies this as a 3.Zug vehicle. The marking system used by this battalion is discussed in detail on page 21 of the illustration section.

1.The town of Novelskij has either been renamed or disappeared since 1944 while Wladisslawtschik was in fact a farm holding and in all likelihood was named for the owner. In any case neither appear on any of the modern maps which I have been able to view and we can only be certain that both were near Monastyryshche, a large town 40 kilometres north-west of Uman.

A mid production Tiger I of Stab, schwere Panzer-Abteilung 507. The other headquarters tanks were numbered A and B and the markings of the company tanks are shown on the back cover. Above are two versions of the Panzer Assault badge, the award for taking part in seventy-five separate armoured attacks and the basic grade awarded for three operations.

SCHWERE PANZER-ABTEILUNG 507

Originally created on 7 May 1943 from personnel of I.Abteilung, Panzer-Regiment 3, the battalion was equipped with Pzkw V Panther tanks and returned on 30 June to 2.Panzer-Division, the regiment's parent formation.

On 23 September a new battalion was raised from I.Abteilung, Panzer-Regiment 4 and after training in Germany and France received its first Tigers on 23 December 1943. The battalion returned to the Eastern Front on 21 March 1944 and was attached to XXXVIII.Panzerkorps near Olesko, approximately 40 kilometres north-east of Lviv. Within twenty-four hours the Tigers were in action and for most of March supported 359.Infanterie-Division in attacks around Slobotda Zlota on the Studenka river. On 29 March the second and third companies were attached to Panzverband Friebe (1) while 1.Kompanie remained with 357.Infanterie-Division near Olejow, now Oliiv, north-west of Ternopil.

During the next five days the Tigers were engaged in attacks on the Soviet positions around Pokropyvna, just off the road from Ternopil to Zboriv, and as a covering force for the units attempting to re-supply the German garrison in Brody, some 60 kilometres to the north-west. By 2 April the operational tanks of the battalion were divided between Panzerverband Friebe with nine, 357.Infanterie-Division with three and 359.Infanterie-Division with seven. On 11 April the Tigers with Panzerverband Friebe began the relief attack towards Ternopil and it was at this time that the tanks were issued with spare tracks that were mounted on the hull front. These are quite obvious in many photographs and supply a convenient, if not wholly accurate, method of dating those images.

Attacking from the north, Friebe's men were unable to make any headway, due in some part at least to the weather, and were ordered to reinforce 9.SS-Panzer-Division Hohenstaufen which had been attacking from the south. Although contact was made with the German garrison on Sunday, 16 April the relief attempts were ultimately unsuccessful and on 19 April 1944 the remaining tanks of the battalion's second and third companies were withdrawn to Taurow, 25 kilometres east of Lodz. During this time 1.Kompanie had been fighting near Brody with 359.Infanterie-Division where eight tanks had been lost. On 8 May 1944 the three companies were reunited at Lemberg, modern Lviv, and placed under the command of 8.Panzer-Division.

On 4 July the battalion was attached to Generalmajor Rudolf Holste's 4.Kavallerie-Brigade taking part in an advance as far as Kletsk, 35 kilometres east of Baranovichi in Belarus, and a counterattack at the

EQUIPMENT ALLOCATIONS AND LOSSES, SCHWERE PANZER-ABTEILUNG 507, 1944

		Jan	Feb	Mar	Apr	May	Jun	Jul	Aug	Sep	Oct	Nov	Dec
s.Pz-Abt 507	Received	3	26	6	12		2	6	12			10*	1
Tiger I	Lost			4	4	8	1	11	13		1		
	On Hand	19	45	47/14	55/32	47/46	48	43	42/13	42/40	41	51	52
	* 6 new tanks and 4 returned from repair.												

1.Although this name is used in most accounts the Kriegstagebuch of XXXXVIII.Panzerkorps actually refers to this ad-hoc formation as Kampfgruppe Friebe and states that it consisted of a single battery of an independent heavy artillery battalion with a bridging column - both corps level units - together with engineer, signals, supply and staff units from 8.Panzer-Division and the twenty-four Panthers of I.Abteilung, Panzer-Regiment 11. There is no mention of either the half-tracks and grenadiers that Panzergrenadier Regiment 8 and Panzergrenadier Regiment 74 supplied or the nine Tigers of schwere Panzer-Abteilung 507 and it is possible that these were attached after 25 March when the entry was made, contrary to Schneider's account.

village of Svajatycy some 14 kilometres to the north-west. By 9 July the Tigers had withdrawn to Slonim, an important road junction on the Isa river, a tributary of the Neman, about 40 kilometres west of Baranovichi. The Germans had managed to hold on to a bridgehead here on the eastern bank of the river and elements of the battalion were attached to Gruppe von Vormann and Gruppe Harteneck (1).

After withdrawing along the Slonim-Bialystock road the battalion supported the tanks of Panzer-Regiment 35 of 4.Panzer-Division and by 31 July had fallen back through Ulezly near Grodno to Svislach in Belarus, 8 kilometres from the present Polish frontier and finally to Podozierany, 40 kilometres east of Bialystok in Poland were the Tigers were formed into a Kampfgruppe with Panzergrenadier-Regiment 35. On the next day however the battalion was detached from 4.Panzer-Division and placed under the Operational control of I.Kavalleriekorps for a counterattack north of Mien on the eastern bank of the Vistula, 20 kilometres south-east of Torun in Poland. Conducting a fighting withdrawal, on 18 August the Tigers crossed the Narev river and for the remainder of the month attempted to hold up the main Soviet offensive in local counterattacks at Zambrow and Czerwony Bor, withdrawing to once again cross the meandering Narev near Napiorki Butne, south of Rozan. On 11 September the battalion was attached to XLVI.Panzerkorps as an operational reserve although an unknown number of Tigers were left with 6.Panzer-Division and six others in the forest south-west of Chrzanowo along the Ciechanow-Rozan road. From 1 November to 14 January 1945 the battalion was held as an operational reserve with XXIII.Armeekorps near Zichenau in East Prussia, now Ciechanow in Poland.

SCHWERE PANZER-ABTEILUNG 509

Established on 9 September 1943 with three companies from surplus personnel of the disbanded Panzer-Regiment 204, the battalion received its first tanks on 30 August of the same year. By 28 October, with its training complete and with a full complement of forty-five Tigers, the battalion entrained for the Eastern Front. On 7 November, 3.Kompanie was thrown into action near the village of Fatovets, north-east of Kolomyia in western Ukraine in support of 2.SS-Panzergrenadier-Division Das Reich while 2.Kompanie was deployed with 25.Panzer-Division between Koziatyn and Skvyra, some 300 kilometres further to the east. The location and activities of 1.Kompanie are unclear at this time but is almost certain that the complete battalion was re-united by 15 November 1943 around the village of Kozhanka on the Kamyanka river south-east of Fastiv where urgent repair work was carried out. During December 1943 the battalion took part in the fighting around Berdychiv in northern Ukraine and on the last day of 1943 lost two Tigers - one irreparably damaged after falling through a bridge and one to an engine fire.

Above, left: Photographed in late 1943 this mid production Tiger I of 3.Kompanie, schwere Panzer-Abteilung 509 can be identified by the very distinctive numbering style used by the battalion at the time. As winter approached and the tanks were camouflaged with whitewash the company numbers were rendered in black in the same style. This may be one of the six tanks the battalion lost on 10 November in an attack on Mirowka led by 3.Kompanie in support of SS-Panzer-Regiment 2 - the only complete losses the battalion suffered before the new year. Of those tanks, two were destroyed by their own crews when it was decided that they could not be recovered and it is tempting to speculate that this Tiger may be one of those. Note the plug on the turret side that replaced the large, bolted pistol port in July 1943 and was subsequently discontinued in the following October. This tank also has the early hull extensions. The marking on the stowage box to the left of the tank's number is a white, rhomboid tactical sign denoting a tracked armour unit. In the original print it is possible to see a small, dark letter G in the centre. The latter may indicate the battalion's commander, Major Gierka, whose previous command, Panzer-Abteilung 215 in Sicily, had marked their white star formation sign with a G in an almost identical style. At right: In early 1944, probably late spring, the numbering system was changed to a much more standardised style with black numbers outlined in white carried on the rear stowage box and the turret sides forward of the vision slits. Of note are the 20ton jack in its bracket on the hull rear and the tubular spare antenna holder on the top edge of the hull.

1.Gruppe von Vormann was made up from the survivors of General Nikolaus von Vormann's 9.Armee. The armoured element came for the most part from 23.Panzer-Division. Gruppe Harteneck - sometimes referred to as Korpsgruppe Harteneck, Kampfgruppe von Harteneck and Gruppe Generalleutnant von Harteneck - was an ad hoc unit commanded by Gustav von Harteneck which also contained, at various times, elements of 4.Panzer-Division, 4.Kavallerie-Brigade, the remnants of 29.Infanterie-Division and Panzer-Abteilung 118 - all units of 2.Armee. Given that schwere Panzer-Abteilung reported that forty-five tanks in total were on hand on 8 July 1944, and nineteen Tigers were attached to Harteneck's command, it is reasonable to assume that the balance went to Vormann.

EQUIPMENT ALLOCATIONS AND LOSSES, SCHWERE PANZER-ABTEILUNG 509, 1944

		Jan	Feb	Mar	Apr	May	Jun	Jul	Aug	Sep	Oct	Nov	Dec
s.Pz-Abt 509	Received		8			28*	15**		6	*On 8 September the battalion left*			
Tiger I	Lost	3	1	5	1	11***	17****	4		*for Germany to re-equip with the*			
	On Hand	28/26	35/28	30	29	46/37	44/33	40	46	*Tiger II, returning in January 1945*			
		* 4 from sPz-Abt 503; ** 9 from sPz-Abt 501; *** Returned to factory; **** 3 returned to factory, 14 to Hungarians											

In early January 1944 the battalion was involved in defensive operations north-east of Vinnitsa in the Ukraine, recapturing the village of Ulanoff near the road to Molochky after several attempts, and near Ljubar where 3.Kompanie supported 1.SS-Panzer-Division. During February the Tigers of the battalion, operating with elements of 291.Infanterie-Division, took part in the attacks to recapture Iziaslav on the Horyn river south-west of Shepetivka. After no less than six attempts, on 23 February, the Tigers and infantrymen of Grenadier-Regiment 54 managed to take the town.

In March the battalion was attached to Panzergruppe von Waldenfels (1) and took part in counterattacks at Kusmin, Lashawa and near Proskurov - present day Khmelnytskyi in western Ukraine - with Panzer-Regiment 6 and Panzer-Regiment 11. The Tigers were involved in the successful assault on Alekseiniez-Polny, probably modern Shevchenka, clearing the road between Yarmolyntsi and Horodok and by the end of the month had established a bridgehead across the Sereth river with Panzergruppe von Breith (2). On 20 April the battalion was moved to Kolomyia on the Prut river were it remained as an operational reserve and was also used as a training unit for Hungarian tank crews training on the Tiger. Fourteen of the battalion's tanks were handed over to the Hungarians in late June (3).

The battalion returned to the front on 18 July to take part in an attack on Krystynopol and Tomaschov finally withdrawing towards Lublin, south-east of Warsaw, just 30 kilometres from the Vistula. During August the battalion took part in the defensive battles in the Vistula bend near Kielce and Sandomierz and on 1 September was attached XXXXVIII.Panzerkorps. On 8 September the remaining tanks were handed over to schwere Panzer-Abteilung 501 and the crews were transferred to Truppenübungsplatz Senne to re-equip with the Tiger II. The battalion did not return to the east until mid-January 1945.

SCHWERE PANZER-ABTEILUNG 510

The last of the army's independent Tiger battalions, this unit was formed on 6 June 1944 by scraping together personnel from the maintenance company of schwere Panzer-Abteilung 504, a number of officers who were training at the company commanders school at Versailles (4) and a draft from Panzer-Ersatz und Ausbildungs-Abteilung 500 stationed at Paderborn in Germany. The battalion's formation and training period was extremely short with the last tanks being delivered on 7 July and schwere Panzer-Abteilung 510 arriving at the front just two weeks later. The battalion went into action for the first time on 26 July 1944 when the Tigers of 1.Kompanie attacked Soviet positions south-east of Kaunas in Lithuania.

At right: A late production Tiger I of 1.Kompanie, schwere Panzer-Abteilung 510. The application of the company numbers could vary greatly from neat to rather amateurish as can be seen in our accompanying photographs. Most, but not all, tanks carried the battalion's unit insignia as shown here.

1. Made up from parts of 6.Panzer-Division.
2. Made up from elements of III.Panzerkorps.
3. Against orders the battalion retained its newer tanks and instead gave the Hungarians its least combat ready vehicles including nine battle weary Tigers taken over from schwere Panzer-Abteilung 503 in May.
4. The Kompanieführerschule für schnelle Truppen, based at Versailles in France, was one of the hundreds of Wehrmacht training establishments scattered throughout Germany and the occupied countries. The school was made up of a staff, a staff company and four instructional companies and undertook the training of potential company commanders specifically for armoured units.

EQUIPMENT ALLOCATIONS AND LOSSES, SCHWERE PANZER-ABTEILUNG 510, 1944

		Jan	Feb	Mar	Apr	May	Jun	Jul	Aug	Sep	Oct	Nov	Dec
s.Pz-Abt 510	Received						27	18	6			6*	
Tiger I	Lost							2	10	1	8	10	4
	On Hand						27	43	39/35	38/33	30/13	26/16	22/18
	From 3.Kompanie, sPz-Abt 502.												

During July the battalion was in action at Kerlupys, probably modern Karciupis also on the outskirts of Kaunas fighting its way to Kulva, almost 25 kilometres north-east of Kaunas on the road to Seta. In August the battalion took part in the counterattack to retake Raseiniai on the Klaipeda-Kaunas road and supported 14.Panzer-division in the defence of Jonelaiciai, further to the north on the other side of the Kurtuvenai forest - today a national park. In September the battalion was attached to XXX.Armeekorps and repulsed the Soviet forces at Kursenai on the Venta river west of Siauliai, an important junction near the Latvian border and the most important town in northern Lithuania, with Grenadier-Regiment 1113 and I.Abteilung of Artillerie-Regiment 1551, both from 551.Grenadier-Division. In October schwere Panzer-Abteilung 510 was attached to Armeeabteilung Grasser (1) and here the battalion, supported by 4.Panzer-Division destroyed the enemy bridgehead across the Venta river near the village of Moscheieken, present day Mazaikiai, some 60 Kilometres north-west of Siauliai. On 16 October with the commencement of the 1st battle of Kurland, 3.Kompanie of schwere Panzer-Abteilung 502 was incorporated into schwere Panzer-Abteilung 510 which was at that time fighting at Priekule in Latvia south of the Saldus-Liepaja road (2). Also at this time the battalion's 1.Kompanie was detached and fighting near Meldzer 10 kilometres from Vainode. November found the surviving tanks supporting the Panthers of Panzer-Regiment 36 and infantrymen of Panzergrenadier-Regiment 94 north of Rudbarzi on the road to Liepaja and the Baltic coast. By the end of 1944, 3.Kompanie had been temporarily deactivated and the remains of the battalion were fighting to open the road south-west of Saldus in Latvia between the villages of Evarzi and Pampaïi.

Although the Tiger was envisaged as a breakthrough weapon, the early deployment of the heavy tank battalions was characterised by the use of individual companies, or even tanks, often separated from each other by considerable distance and attached to higher formations whose officers who had little or no understanding of armoured operations. During the winter of 1942-43, in an effort to develop an effective tactical doctrine, the Tiger battalions that reached the front were attached to Panzer divisions with the intention that they should operate as a third battalion of the division's armoured regiment. This arrangement enjoyed only mixed success and it was only after consultation with the commanders in the field that it was decided that the Tiger battalions could be best used if their firepower was massed, operating independently under their own commanders - although, as we have seen, this seldom happened in practice. In addition, it was decided that the Panzer regiments of the three armoured divisions of the Waffen-SS and the army's Grossdeutschland division should be reinforced with an organic heavy tank company.

PANZER-REGIMENT GROSSDEUTSCHLAND

As a fully motorised infantry formation the Grossdeutschland division had received a tank battalion in early 1942 comprising a staff and three medium tank companies. In January 1943 the battalion was upgraded to a full regiment with a second battalion formed from II.Abteilung, Panzer-Regiment 203 with three medium companies equipped with Pzkw III and Pzkw IV tanks. The original tank battalion was renamed I.Abteilung, Panzer-Regiment Grossdeutschland on 3 March 1943 when the second battalion reached the front.

Also attached to the second battalion was the newly raised heavy company. Created on 5 February 1943 from 3.Kompanie, Panzer-Regiment 203 and named 13.Kompanie, Panzer-Regiment Grossdeutschland (3), the company arrived in Russia in late February with just nine Tigers. On 1 July 1943 the company was renamed 9.Kompanie, Panzer-Regiment Grossdeutschland and took part in Operation Citadel without the loss of a single tank, although a number were badly in need of repair. At the same time the third companies of both schwere-Panzer Abteilung 501 and schwere-Panzer Abteilung 504 were incorporated into the regiment, fully equipped, as the tenth and eleventh companies of a new III.Abteilung. The new companies would not rejoin the battalion until 14 August 1943 by which time 9.Kompanie had just one combat ready Tiger. During the remainder of 1943 the battalion was engaged in the fighting around Karachev near Bryansk in Russia and in the defensive battles around Akhtyrka in present day Ukraine. The battalion took part in the fighting for the Kremenchuk bridgehead on the river Dnieper, north-west of Dnepropetrovsk, losing four Tigers in a single day. By this time the battalion's material losses were so severe that tank crews were sent to fight as infantry, reinforcing Grenadier-Regiment Grossdeutschland. By the end of the year the battalion, with thirteen operational tanks, was preparing to defend Kirovograd.

In early January 1944 the battalion was engaged in the defensive battles west of Kirovograd in central Ukraine and in the following weeks the Tigers were attached to Panzergruppe Bayer operating in support of 11.Panzer-Division in attacks against the Russian positions around the Tscherkassy Pocket until the end

....*continued on page 52*

1. Formed from Armmeabteilung Narva in September 1944 which had been made up of elements of II.Armeekorps and III.(Germanisches) SS-Panzerkorps and scratch Kriegsmarine units.
2. Not to be confused with Priekule, south of Klaipeda, in Lithuania. Liepaja was renamed from Libau in 1945.
3. Sources differ on this date with Jentz giving 13 February 1943 while Schneider suggests the date shown here stating that it was the consequence of an order which originated with the headquarters of Wehrkreis III although he does not give the order number as he often does with other formations. Almost all agree, however, that the first tanks were not allocated before February 1943.

PzKpfw Tiger ausf E. 11.Kompanie, III.Abteilung, Panzer-Regiment Grossdeutschland. Ukraine. January 1944. A small number of these tanks were built during July and August 1943 and featured a mixture of early and mid production features including the two headlights on the hull front, the early road wheels, the complete Feifel air filtering system and the forward opening hatch of the cast cupola. These details are discussed further in the technical section. Other photographs of this tank show the pistol port plug on the left side of the turret fitted from July 1943 and the lack of Zimmerit which further limits the time frame to pre-September.

Above: This may be the Tiger I numbered C11 and commanded by Oberleutnant Leusing which was destroyed near Wirballen - modern Virbalis in Lithuania - on 6 August 1944 in a firefight with a strong Soviet armoured force including a number of JS-2 heavy tanks.

PzKpfw Tiger ausf E. 9.Kompanie, III.Abteilung, Panzer-Regiment Grossdeutschland. Romania. Summer 1944. Photographed at Vaslui in eastern Romania in early June 1944 as the company was entraining for shipment to East Prussia, this tank's camouflage and markings are typical of the battalion's Tigers throughout the summer months of 1944. The series of photographs on which this illustration is based show clearly the steel-rimmed, resilient road wheels introduced in February 1944 and the monocular gun sight, not visible here, incorporated in March. Although difficult to be certain the turret appears to lack the socket mounts fitted to the hull roof in June 1944 suggesting that this tank is probably one of the six Tigers received by III.Abteilung on 20 April, bringing the operational total to twenty. The method of numbering each tank did not follow the usual, three-digit system and instead the battalion's 9th, 10th and 11th companies used A, B and C respectively with the platoon and individual vehicle identified by the following number. The headquarters tanks were numbered S01, S02 and S03. There is evidence to suggest that at least some of these numbers were rendered in white with a black outline by the end of the year. Our photograph shows the Balkenkreuz on both the hull side and rear.

PzKpfw Tiger ausf E. 2.Kompanie, schwere Panzer-Abteilung 501. Byelorussia. Winter 1943-44. Photographed during the battles along the Dnieper in the Orscha region of what is today Belarus, this tank is probably one of the mid production models the battalion received in November 1943. This unit used the official three-digit numbering system to identify its tanks, the numbers rendered as a black outline only with the whitewash camouflage carefully painted around the edges. Note that the number on the rear stowage box appears to have been painted over the whitewash and this seems to have been common, if not universal. Also note the barbed wire fixed to the exhaust covers. Almost all the tanks of this battalion had their hulls covered with wire to some degree, most far more extensively than shown here, presumably to deter or impede tank-hunting Russian infanytrmen.

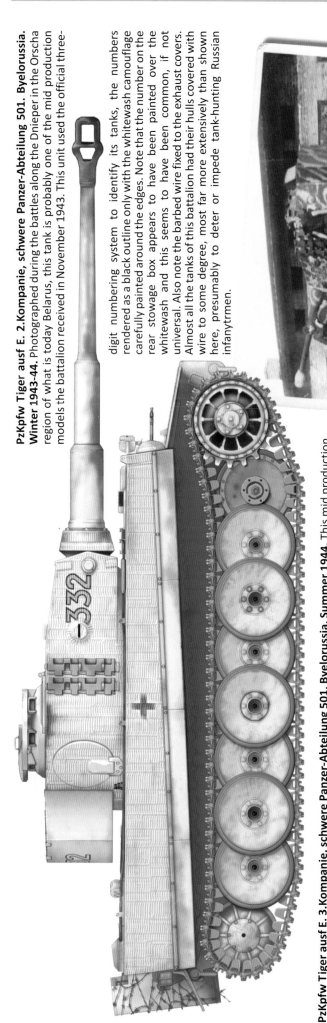

PzKpfw Tiger ausf E. 3.Kompanie, schwere Panzer-Abteilung 501. Byelorussia. Summer 1944. This mid production model was built between August 1943, when the single headlight at the hull front was introduced into production, and some time before October when the pistol port on the turret side was discontinued. The turret number, as can be seen from our photograph, is a decidedly darker shade than the base coat of Dunkelgelb confirming that not all the tanks of this battalion had their numbers rendered as a black outline only. Although it is impossible to determine the colour with any certainty it is rendered here as Olivgrün, which is at least possible. Several photographs of this tank exist and the image shown at right is probably the earliest, made during April or May 1944 when the battalion received a large store of spare parts

and was able to repair all its damaged tanks. This would explain the apparently fresh camouflage scheme and the dark coloured replacement gun barrel, almost certainly painted in RAL 7021 Schwartzgrau. In what we can safely assume to be the last photograph made of this Tiger, abandoned by the roadside while German prisoners are marched past, little has changed with the exception of the kill rings on the barrel. Damage is limited to the mudguards and fenders and the engine access door has been left open. In his account of the battalion's history Wolfgang Schneider lists the number of tanks lost in June and July stating that all were completely destroyed either by enemy action or by their own crews with the exception of one Tiger which was abandoned on 4 July 1944, some 20 kilometres east of Minsk after breaking down. Although we can never be certain it is tempting to speculate that this may be the same tank.

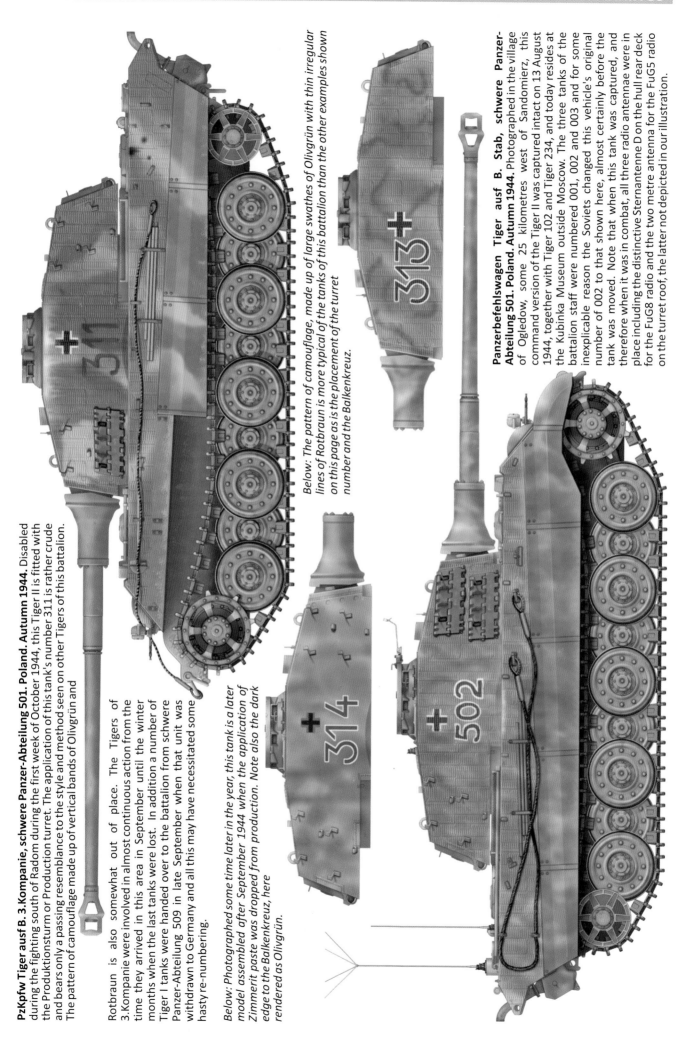

PzKpfw Tiger ausf B. 3.Kompanie, schwere Panzer-Abteilung 501. Poland. Autumn 1944. Disabled during the fighting south of Radom during the first week of October 1944, this Tiger II is fitted with the Produktionsturm or Production turret. The application of this tank's number 311 is rather crude and bears only a passing resemblance to the style and method seen on other Tigers of this battalion. The pattern of camouflage made up of vertical bands of Olivgrün and

Rotbraun is also somewhat out of place. The Tigers of 3.Kompanie were involved in almost continuous action from the time they arrived in this area in September until the winter months when the last tanks were lost. In addition a number of Tiger I tanks were handed over to the battalion from schwere Panzer-Abteilung 509 in late September when that unit was withdrawn to Germany and all this may have necessitated some hasty re-numbering.

Below: Photographed some time later in the year, this tank is a later model assembled after September 1944 when the application of Zimmerit paste was dropped from production. Note also the dark edge to the Balkenkreuz, here rendered as Olivgrün.

Below: The pattern of camouflage, made up of large swathes of Olivgrün with thin irregular lines of Rotbraun is more typical of the tanks of this battalion than the other examples shown on this page as is the placement of the turret number and the Balkenkreuz.

Panzerbefehlswagen Tiger ausf B. Stab, schwere Panzer-Abteilung 501. Poland. Autumn 1944. Photographed in the village of Ogledow, some 25 kilometres west of Sandomierz, this command version of the Tiger II was captured intact on 13 August 1944, together with Tiger 102 and Tiger 234, and today resides at the Kubinka Museum outside Moscow. The three tanks of the battalion staff were numbered 001, 002 and 003 and for some inexplicable reason the Soviets changed this vehicle's original number of 002 to that shown here, almost certainly before the tank was moved. Note that when this tank was captured, and therefore when it was in combat, all three radio antennae were in place including the distinctive Sternantenne D on the hull rear deck for the FuG8 radio and the two metre antenna for the FuG5 radio on the turret roof, the latter not depicted in our illustration.

19

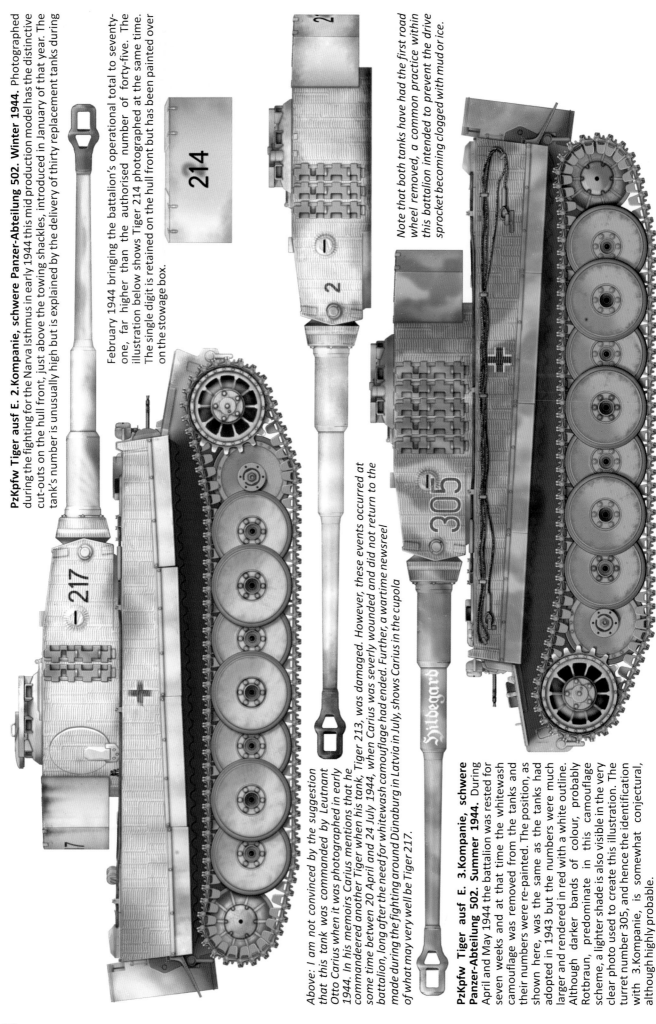

PzKpfw Tiger ausf E. 2.Kompanie, schwere Panzer-Abteilung 502. Winter 1944. Photographed during the fighting for the Narva Isthmus in early 1944 this mid production model has the distinctive cut-outs on the hull front, just above the towing shackles, introduced in January of that year. The tank's number is unusually high but is explained by the delivery of thirty replacement tanks during February 1944 bringing the battalion's operational total to seventy-one, far higher than the authorised number of forty-five. The illustration below shows Tiger 214 photographed at the same time. The single digit is retained on the hull front but has been painted over on the stowage box.

Above: I am not convinced by the suggestion that this tank was commanded by Leutnant Otto Carius when it was photographed in early 1944. In his memoirs Carius mentions that he commandeered another Tiger when his tank, Tiger 213, was damaged. However, these events occurred at some time betwen 20 April and 24 July 1944, when Carius was severly wounded and did not return to the battalion, long after the need for whitewash camouflage had ended. Further, a wartime newsreel made during the fighting around Dünaburg in Latvia in July, shows Carius in the cupola of what may very well be Tiger 217.

PzKpfw Tiger ausf E. 3.Kompanie, schwere Panzer-Abteilung 502. Summer 1944. During April and May 1944 the battalion was rested for seven weeks and at that time the whitewash camouflage was removed from the tanks and their numbers were re-painted. The position, as shown here, was the same as the tanks had adopted in 1943 but the numbers were much larger and rendered in red with a white outline. Although darker bands of colour, probably Rotbraun, predominate in this camouflage scheme, a lighter shade is also visible in the very clear photo used to create this illustration. The turret number 305, and hence the identification with 3.Kompanie, is somewhat conjectural, although highly probable.

Note that both tanks have had the first road wheel removed, a common practice within this battalion intended to prevent the drive sprocket becoming clogged with mud or ice.

20

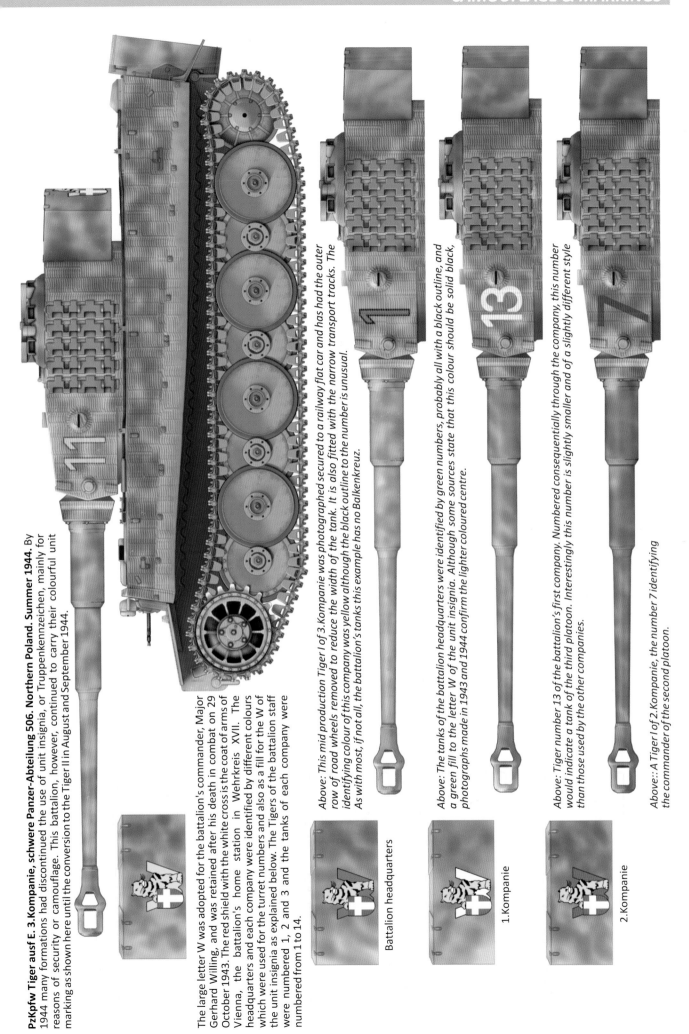

PzKpfw Tiger ausf E. 3.Kompanie, schwere Panzer-Abteilung 506. Northern Poland. Summer 1944. By 1944 many formations had discontinued the use of unit insignia, or Truppenkennzeichen, mainly for reasons of security or camouflage. This battalion, however, continued to carry their colourful unit marking as shown here until the conversion to the Tiger II in August and September 1944.

The large letter W was adopted for the battalion's commander, Major Gerhard Willing, and was retained after his death in combat on 29 October 1943. The red shield with the white cross is the coat of arms of Vienna, the battalion's home station in Wehrkreis XVII. The headquarters and each company were identified by different colours which were used for the turret numbers and also as a fill for the W of the unit insignia as explained below. The Tigers of the battalion staff were numbered 1, 2 and 3 and the tanks of each company were numbered from 1 to 14.

Above: This mid production Tiger I of 3.Kompanie was photographed secured to a railway flat car and has had the outer row of road wheels removed to reduce the width of the tank. It is also fitted with the narrow transport tracks. The identifying colour of this company was yellow although the black outline to the number is unusual. As with most, if not all, the battalion's tanks this example has no Balkenkreuz.

Above: The tanks of the battalion headquarters were identified by green numbers, probably all with a black outline, and a green fill to the letter W of the unit insignia. Although some sources state that this colour should be solid black, photographs made in 1943 and 1944 confirm the lighter coloured centre.

Battalion headquarters

Above: Tiger number 13 of the battalion's first company. Numbered consequentially through the company, this number would indicate a tank of the third platoon. Interestingly this number is slightly smaller and of a slightly different style than those used by the other companies.

1.Kompanie

Above:: A Tiger I of 2.Kompanie, the number 7 identifying the commander of the second platoon.

2.Kompanie

PzKpfw Tiger ausf E. Schwere Panzer-Abteilung 503. Poland. Spring 1944. In February, when the battalion was attached to Panzer-Regiment Bäke, a small detachment under Leutnant Günter Piepgras from 1.Kompanie was sent to Germany to pick up twelve replacement Tigers and return to the front. Arriving at Lemberg, present day Lviv in Ukraine, on 23 February they

were unable to rejoin the battalion and were instead attached to Kampfgruppe Mittermeier under the overall command of 359.Infanterie-Division. In a complete departure from the battalion's normal practice of identifying its tanks with black numbers outlined in white, the tanks were marked with a peculiar mixture of large numbers, rendered in different styles, in either red or black with the company command using 100 and 101, later changed to 101 and 102, while the first platoon were numbered from 111 to 115 and the second with 121 to 125. Photographed near Berezhany, just west of Lviv, the vehicle shown at right is without doubt one of Leutnant Piepgras' Tigers although the turret number contains just two digits. Photographs exist showing tanks of this unit without any identifying number and it may be that the turret numbers were added in stages after the tanks arrived in the East. Although this tank is depicted here a light, mottled camouflage of Rotbraun and Olivgrün over the Dunkelgelb base colour, it may have merely been discoloured with dust and grease.

PzKpfw Tiger ausf E. Schwere Panzer-Abteilung 503. Poland. Spring 1944. All twelve Tigers of Leutnant Piepgras' command were late production models fitted with the resilient steel road wheels that were incorporated into production in February 1944. The example shown at left, however, retains the earlier form of hull extensions which were supposed to have been phased out in January when the distinctive notched versions were introduced. It is also obvious that there is no provision for the shovel on the glacis, a

feature discontinued in January 1944. The placement of the Balkenkreuz national insignia was common throughout the company. The darker colour of the barrel is quite clear in our photograph indicating what is probably a recent replacement. It is also clear that this tank has no disruptive camouflage pattern and has been left in its base coat of Dunkelgelb. In early May the surviving nine tanks, manned by personnel from 3.Kompanie, were transferred to 1.Tiger-Lehrkompanie of 1.Panzerlehrgruppe Nordukraine, an instructional unit, and tasked with training Hungarian army tank crews on the Tiger. Photographs show that the numbering sequence was retained but the numbers appear to have been re-painted, probably in black, maintaining the size and position of the originals but in a consistent style. It is also possible that the tanks retained their old numbers.

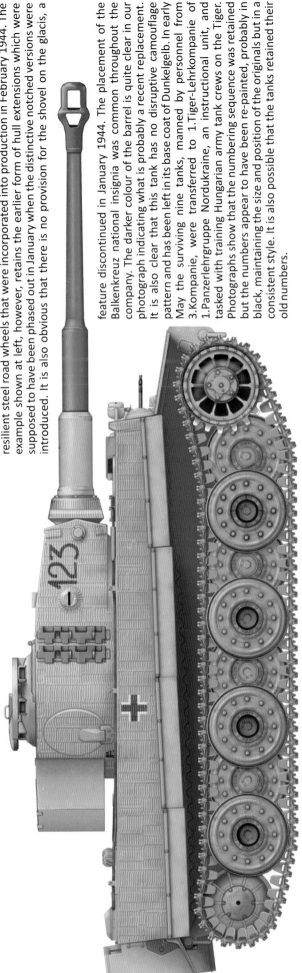

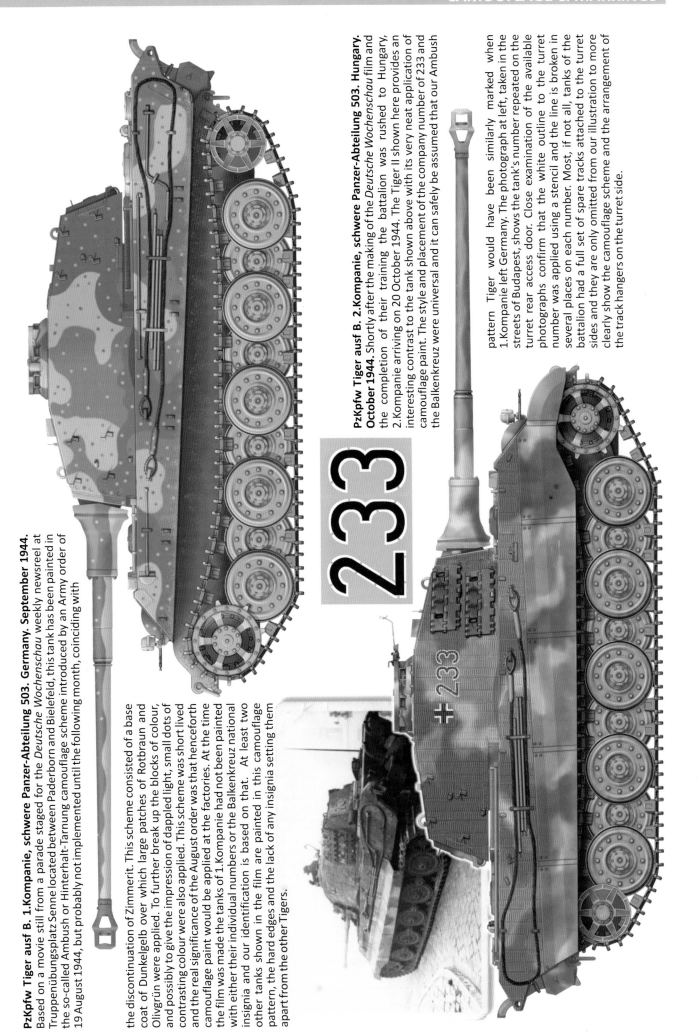

PzKpfw Tiger ausf B. 1.Kompanie, schwere Panzer-Abteilung 503. Germany. September 1944.
Based on a movie still from a parade staged for the *Deutsche Wochenschau* weekly newsreel at Truppenübungsplatz Senne located between Paderborn and Bielefeld, this tank has been painted in the so-called Ambush or Hinterhalt-Tarnung camouflage scheme introduced by an Army order of 19 August 1944, but probably not implemented until the following month, coinciding with

the discontinuation of Zimmerit. This scheme consisted of a base coat of Dunkelgelb over which large patches of Rotbraun and Olivgrün were applied. To further break up the blocks of colour, and possibly to give the impression of dappled light, small dots of contrasting colour were also applied. This scheme was short lived and the real significance of the August order was that henceforth camouflage paint would be applied at the factories. At the time the film was made the tanks of 1.Kompanie had not been painted with either their individual numbers or the Balkenkreuz national insignia and our identification is based on that. At least two other tanks shown in the film are painted in this camouflage pattern, the hard edges and the lack of any insignia setting them apart from the other Tigers.

PzKpfw Tiger ausf B. 2.Kompanie, schwere Panzer-Abteilung 503. Hungary. October 1944. Shortly after the making of the *Deutsche Wochenschau* film and the completion of their training the battalion was rushed to Hungary, 2.Kompanie arriving on 20 October 1944. The Tiger II shown here provides an interesting contrast to the tank shown above with its very neat application of camouflage paint. The style and placement of the company number of 233 and the Balkenkreuz were universal and it can safely be assumed that our Ambush

pattern Tiger would have been similarly marked when 1.Kompanie left Germany. The photograph at left, taken in the streets of Budapest, shows the tank's number repeated on the turret rear access door. Close examination of the available photographs confirm that the white outline to the turret number was applied using a stencil and the line is broken in several places on each number. Most, if not all, tanks of the battalion had a full set of spare tracks attached to the turret sides and they are only omitted from our illustration to more clearly show the camouflage scheme and the arrangement of the track hangers on the turret side.

23

PzKpfw Tiger ausf E. 2.Kompanie, schwere Panzer-Abteilung 505. Ukraine. Winter 1943-44. This tank was almost certainly built in June 1943 after the smoke candle dischargers were dropped from production and before the new cast cupola was introduced in the following month. Other noticeable features are the fittings for twin headlights on the hull front, although the actual lights are missing, the bolted pistol port on the turret side, discontinued in June 1943 and the full set of Feifel air cleaning components.

The box fixed to the stowage bin is a field modification and was commonly seen on the battalion's tanks at this time. Another field modification was the bracket on either side at the hull front holding spare track links, or at least in one case heavy, iron clevises (see photograph on page 10). The large, sturdy unditching beam is held in place by three metal struts welded to the hull side. The battalion's striking unit insignia of a charging knight and the tank's company number 231 has been carefully applied over the whitewash camouflage. It is likely that this Tiger is one of the tanks the battalion received in late June or mid-July 1943.

At right: A thin, metal command pennant said to have been found near Königsberg. Although of uncertain provenance it is possibly the best indication we have of what were, officially at least, the colours used for the battalion insignia.

At left: The battalion's unit insignia. There is no real evidence to suggest that different colours were used to identify the individual companies and battalion headquarters, although the idea has been proposed so often that it is now widely accepted as fact. The many available contemporary photographs show clearly that the horse's barding, the helmet crest and the pennon of the same badge could be of decidedly different shades and it is likely that any suitable colour was used.

PzKpfw Tiger ausf E. 2.Kompanie, schwere Panzer-Abteilung 505. Poland. Summer 1944. This late production model was built at some time in February 1944 when the steel road wheels were introduced into production. Not visible here, but clearly shown in other photographs, is the binocular gun sight which was not phased out until the following month.

Other features include the single headlight at the centre of the hull front incorporated into production in January 1944 and the notched hull extension introduced in the same month. Although the camouflage pattern as applied to these tanks is often described as Rotbraun bands on the Dunkelgelb base, there is evidence of a third shade in the very clear photographs on which this illustration is based and which is here rendered as Olivgrün. Note that a large patch of Zimmerit has been removed to accommodate the battalion's insignia. The yellow band on the barrel, highlighting the tank's number, was common to this unit's Tiger I tanks. Again a sturdy unditching beam is carried.

PzKpfw Tiger ausf B. 1.Kompanie, schwere Panzer-Abteilung 505. Germany. Summer 1944. Photographed with its crew shortly before the battalion left Truppenübungsplatz Ohrdruf near Weimar in central Germany for the Eastern Front on Friday 8 September 1944, this tank is typical of the forty-five Tigers on hand at the time. A large patch of zimmerit has been removed from the turret side to accommodate the battalion's unit insignia which has also been avoided by the wide bands of Rotbraun and Olivgrün camouflage.

The numbering system shown here was consistent throughout the battalion with the larger number on the gun mantlet identifying the company and the numbers on the barrel indicating the platoon and individual vehicle.

At left: Feldwebel Kronke's Tiger II number 124 showing the Bosch headlight attached to the gun mantlet. A second, identical headlight was fixed to the right side. Note the rack holding the gun cleaning rods welded to the hull just below the bracket where the headlight is normally placed and what is presumably a hand hold just behind the left front fender, both field modifications. Barely visible is the small cut-out lucky charm attached by wire to the bolts of the gun mantlet, based on the Brothers Grimm story of Hans im Glück, or Hans in Luck. A further, clearer photograph has enabled us to recreate the figure here although of course the colours can only be guesswork.

PzKpfw Tiger ausf B. 1.Kompanie, schwere Panzer-Abteilung 505. East Prussia. Autumn 1944. Commanded by Feldwebel Horst Kronke, this Tiger is almost certainly one of the thirty-nine vehicles received by the battalion during the last weeks of August 1944. The gun mantlet does not have the bracket for the poison gas detector suggesting that that this tank was assembled prior to July. The Bosch headlight was removed from its bracket on the hull front, the light's conduit was also neatly removed, and two headlights were mounted on the upper edge of the gun mantlet. This modification was carried out with at least some other tanks of this battalion and photographs exist which show the bracket on the mantlet, less the light, on Tiger 202 and Tiger 302. The tank's number as seen here reads correctly as 124 and some confusion has occurred when the numbers are viewed from the left hand side where the company is placed last in line. All the battalion's Tigers used a black number with a white outline as shown here and the number was repeated on the turret rear access door. The Tigers of the battalion headquarters were numbered I, II and III, the number appearing on the gun mantlet. Note that the camouflage of Rotbraun and Olivgrün must have been applied while the towing cable and gun cleaning rods were in place on the hull side leaving their outline in Dunkelgelb.

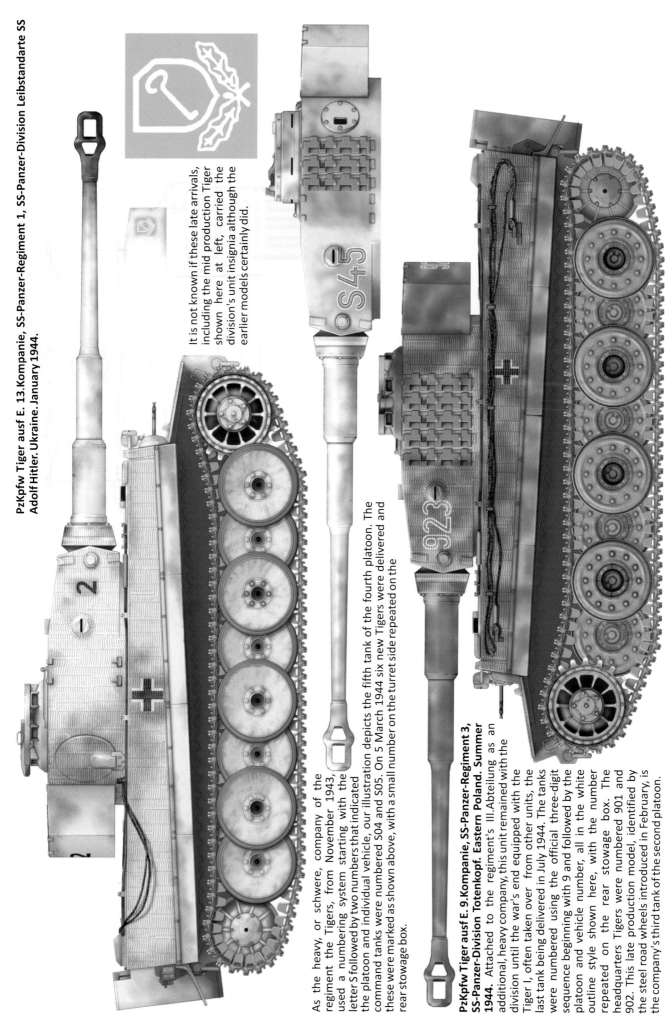

PzKpfw Tiger ausf E. 13.Kompanie, SS-Panzer-Regiment 1, SS-Panzer-Division Leibstandarte SS Adolf Hitler. Ukraine. January 1944.

It is not known if these late arrivals, including the mid production Tiger shown here at left, carried the division's unit insignia although the earlier models certainly did.

As the heavy, or schwere, company of the regiment the Tigers, from November 1943, used a numbering system starting with the letter S followed by two numbers that indicated the platoon and individual vehicle, our illustration depicts the fifth tank of the fourth platoon. The command tanks were numbered S04 and S05. On 5 March 1944 six new Tigers were delivered and these were marked as shown above, with a small number on the turret side repeated on the rear stowage box.

PzKpfw Tiger ausf E. 9.Kompanie, SS-Panzer-Regiment 3, SS-Panzer-Division Totenkopf. Eastern Poland. Summer 1944. Attached to the regiment's III.Abteilung as an additional, heavy company, this unit remained with the division until the war's end equipped with the Tiger I, often taken over from other units, the last tank being delivered in July 1944. The tanks were numbered using the official three-digit sequence beginning with 9 and followed by the platoon and vehicle number, all in the white outline style shown here, with the number repeated on the rear stowage box. The headquarters Tigers were numbered 901 and 902. This late production model, identified by the steel road wheels introduced in February, is the company's third tank of the second platoon.

26

Pzkfw TIGER I

13.KOMPANIE, SS-PANZER-REGIMENT 1

1/35 Scale

DENNIS WONG

Dennis has used the Tamiya early production kit to represent the tank commanded by SS-Untersturmführer Michael Wittman during the winter battles of 1943-44. These early versions were characterised by the cylindrical commander's cupola, the rubber-tyred, dished wheels and the smoke candle dischargers on the turret sides introduced into production in August 1942 and discontinued in June 1943.

Above: Wittman, at far left, and his crew are congratulated by SS-Obersturmbannfuhrer Peiper, the regimental commander

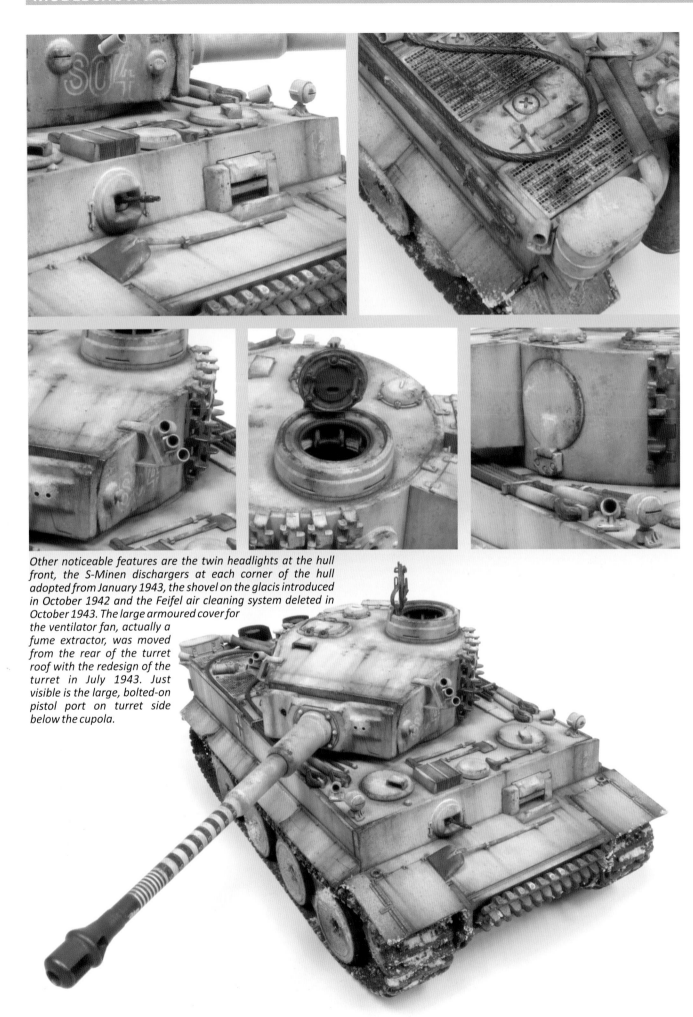

Other noticeable features are the twin headlights at the hull front, the S-Minen dischargers at each corner of the hull adopted from January 1943, the shovel on the glacis introduced in October 1942 and the Feifel air cleaning system deleted in October 1943. The large armoured cover for the ventilator fan, actually a fume extractor, was moved from the rear of the turret roof with the redesign of the turret in July 1943. Just visible is the large, bolted-on pistol port on turret side below the cupola.

Pzkfw TIGER I

SCHWERE PANZER-ABTEILUNG 507
1/35 Scale
DINESH NED

Dinesh's Dragon Models late production Tiger I represents a tank of 3.Kompanie during the defence of East Prussia in November 1944 when this battalion was reduced to twelve serviceable tanks. These late production models are most easily identified by the steel road wheels that were introduced from February 1944. Although absent in our photograph, the spare tracks fixed to either side of the hull front were a common feature of this battalion's tanks.

Other interesting items include the cast cupola introduced in July 1943, complete with AA machine gun mount, the centre headlight on hull front standardised in October 1943, the 20 ton jack in its bracket on the hull rear plate issued from January 1944 and the monocular gun sight incorporated into production from March 1944.

Just visible on the turret roof are the three sockets or Pilze for the jib boom which would date this tank's assembly to June 1944 at the earliest.

Pzkfw TIGER I
SCHWERE PANZER-ABTEILUNG 506
1/35 Scale
DENNIS WONG

Dennis has completed his Tamiya mid production Tiger I in what must have been one of the most colourful unit markings of all the Tiger battalions. The mid production version retained some features of the early models and initiated some of the design aspects that would characterise the later variants. At the top of the page is the cover of the Tigerfibel, the German Army's training manual issued to Tiger crews from 1944.

At left and below: The battalion's impressive unit insignia. Its application and colours are discussed fully in the illustration section.

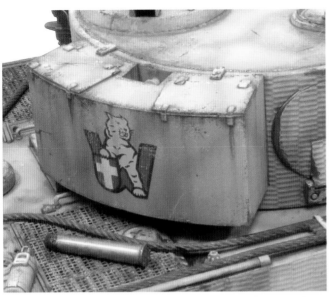

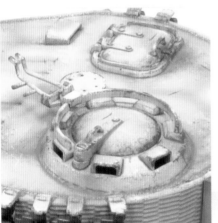

The ventilator cover on turret roof has been moved from the turret rear to a position directly over the breech of the main gun and the cylindrical cupola has been replaced by the cast version. While the older style wheels and the shovel on the glacis have been retained, the headlight was moved to the centre front of the hull from October 1943 and a travel lock for the main gun was added to the rear hull at the right side from the following month.

Finally this tank has the 20 ton jack adopted from January 1944. The practice of removing the first road wheel was common in Russia, particularly in the winter and spring and was intended to prevent ice and mud clogging the drive sprocket.

Pzkfw TIGER I
SCHWERE PANZER-ABTEILUNG 505
1/35 Scale
LIM KIAN GUAN

Lim's model of a 3.Kompanie vehicle fighting in Poland during the summer months is based on the Tamiya late production Tiger I. The category of late production is generally applied to Tigers assembled from February 1944 when the resilient steel road wheels replaced the rubber-rimmed, dished versions.

Interestingly this tank retains the binocular gun sight which was dropped from production in March 1944 narrowing the time frame considerably for this particular vehicle's assembly. The later pattern tracks with chevrons available from October 1943 are clearly visible here. At left: Although space prevented a comprehensive coverage of available crew figures I have included one of my personal favourites here from Evolution Miniatures.

Features initiated in the mid production model are evident here such as the cast cupola and the single headlight at the centre of the hull. The 20 ton jack was incorporated into production in January 1944 and the shovel and its brackets were removed in the same month. The spare tracks on the turret and their hangers, five on the left hand side and two on the right, were introduced in April 1943 before the last of the early production Tiger I tanks were assembled.

Sturmpanzer VI
STURMTIGER
1/35 Scale
DIMITRIS IONNIDIS

Known by a variety of unofficial names, the correct designation for these impressive self-propelled guns is Sturmmörserwagen 606/4 mit 38 cm RW 61. Very few were completed and fewer still were used in the East, in fact just the prototype and a single production vehicle which were sent to Warsaw in August 1944. The model shown here depicts a vehicle in the later stages of construction. A surviving example, said to be the prototype vehicle reworked with a steel fighting compartment and later road wheels as shown here, is on display at the Kubinka Tank Museum near Moscow.

37

For this build Dimitris used the 1/35 scale kit from AFV Club, adding a resin barrel and photo-etched grills from the Voyager Model upgrade set. The metal tracks are from Friulmodel. In order to depict a vehicle as it might have appeared on the assembly line the construction was limited to the basic parts. Further, the colour scheme was restricted for the most part to red primer for the hull while a few wheels were painted yellow for contrast. Paints used were Tamiya acrylics weathered with pigments from AK Interactive, and Uschi van den Rosten with filters and effects from Adam Wilder. A simple white pencil was used for the chalk markings. Finally, the tracks were blackened with Uschi van den Rosten burnishing agent, and weathered with AK Interactive pigments.

Pzkfw TIGER II
SCHWERE PANZER-ABTEILUNG 503
1/35 Scale
SHENG HUI

This beautifully built and painted model depicts one of the two Tigers fitted with the Porsche turret that schwere Panzer-Abteilung 503 had on hand when the battalion returned to the Eastern front in late 1944. The photograph at right shows the actual vehicle during the winter of 1944-45. Modeller Sheng Hui is the brains behind ROCHM Model and his products can be seen on page 47.

Considering that the Tigers are arguably the most famous armoured vehicles ever to take to the battlefield, it should come as no surprise that models of these tanks have been produced by every major manufacturer, and many minor and less well known companies, over the years. Although the early offerings were somewhat basic and often inaccurate, some are still in production today, attesting to the popularity of these large, powerful tanks. The majority of the more recent models are highly detailed replicas, increasingly featuring photo-etched parts and other so-called after market items as standard, often depicting variants which were operational for just a short period of time or which may have only taken part in a single action. The proliferation of models from the major manufacturers has seen the emergence of smaller, specialised companies producing additional items in resin, photo-etched metal and other materials allowing a level of super-detailing which is only limited by the modellers expertise and, of course, budget. Models of the Tiger variants are produced in a number of scales from tiny 6mm wargames miniatures to the huge, radio-controlled 1/6 scale versions. These are, however, at the extreme ends of the market and we have chosen to concentrate on the most popular modelling scales here, 1/35, 1/48 and 1/72. In addition, this list is far from exhaustive, mostly due to reasons of space and almost constant new releases and we would encourage readers to undertake their own research into the areas that interest them most. An index of manufacturers can be found on page 64. Similarly I have limited any comment or critique of these kits or products to those of which I have first hand knowledge.

DRAGON MODELS LTD

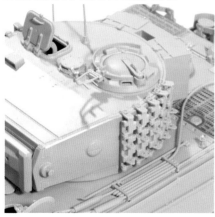  

At the time of writing this Hong Kong based company's catalogue showed forty-six models of Tiger I and II variants in 1/35 and 1/72 scale including kits of the Sturmtiger and Bergetiger recovery vehicle. That number does not include the Jagdtiger tank destroyer which of course did not take part in the fighting in the East. In addition they produce a number of the same tanks, pre-painted and assembled, in 1/144 scale and a complete range of 1/72 scale tanks, again pre-painted and assembled. To complement the vehicles there is a large range of highly detailed, plastic multi-pose figures.

Above: Dragon's Kit 6730 early production Tiger I showing the box art and the assembled model. At the centre of the page is the late production Tiger I, 3 in 1 Kit number 6406.

Above: Dragon Models kit number 6383 Tiger I late production model with Zimmerit in 1/35 scale. The water slide transfers supplied with the kit, and with all Dragon models, are produced by Cartograf of Italy. Option 4, for tank number 933, depicts a Tiger I from the same unit as the tank shown in our illustration section on page 26 and depicts a Tiger I of 9.Kompanie, SS-Panzer-Regiment 3. Shown here in detail are the interior of the radio operator's hatch, later style drive sprocket introduced in May 1943, the engine air exhaust louvres and the mantlet of the main gun complete with Zimmerit texture.

Above: Three examples of Dragon Models 1/72 scale kits. The models of the Armour Pro range are construction kits and should not be confused with the assembled and pre-painted tanks and other armoured vehicles of the company's Dragon Armour range. At left and below are Dragon's mid-production Tiger I and the Henschel turret version of the Tiger II both in 1/72 scale and both enhanced by the highly detailed photo-etched brass sets from E.T. Models. At far left is the sheet of water slide transfers that accompany the Tiger I late production kit. Also printed in Italy by Cartograf, it is very similar to that which is included in the 1/35 scale kit and shown at the top of this page.

41

Above and right: The 1/72 and 1/35 scale versions of the same tank the Tiger II with the Production turret.

Above: From time to time models are re-released as special editions with unique options such as this kit commemorating Gefreiter Alfred Kurzmaul who served with schwere Panzer-Abteilung 503.

TAMIYA

Interestingly Tamiya Inc. began life as a sawmill and timber supply company which also produced wooden ship and aeroplane models as a sideline. These proved so profitable that the company eventually devoted itself to model making and in 1959 began working in plastic, releasing Tamiya's first tank, a Panther, in 1961. By the early 1970s Tamiya was producing a large range of armoured vehicles, figures and accesories and was almost solely responsible for the rise in popularity of 1/35 scale. For their day the kits were highly detailed and accurate, but relatively easy to assemble and affordable. The company's near monopoly of the

market remained unchallenged until the release of the first Dragon Models kits in 1987. In 2003 Tamiya began releasing a series of models in 1/48 scale and this line has been extremely successful for the company, combining the potential for a high level of detail without the expense of the bigger kits. At the time of writing Tamiya produces in 1/35 scale early, mid-production and late versions of the Tiger I, a Tiger II fitted with the Production turret and coated with Zimmerit , a later Tiger II without the Zimmerit and marketed as King Tiger Ardennes Front, a Tiger II with the earlier Porsche turret and a Sturmtiger.

The Tamiya early production Tiger I kit in 1/16 scale. These large models have spawned a complete industry that produces upgrade parts such as the later-style cupola at far left made by Mato.

In 1/48 scale the Tamiya catalogue includes early and late production models of the Tiger I and the Tiger II, the latter with both the Porsche and Production turret. The packaging of the 1/48 scale Late Production Tiger I is shown above while the built and painted model is shown at right. Also shown at the top of the page are shots of the unpainted model showing clearly the level of detail. Below are three example of Tamiya's 1/35 scale Tiger I models all of which are currently available.

Tamiya also produces a range of accessory kits such as the workable King Tiger tracks shown here, brass ammunition for the 8.8cm guns of both the Tiger I and Tiger II and photo-etched brass sets. Above, at right is shown the 1/35 scale King Tiger with Production turret. Below are three of the company's current kits of the Tiger II.

43

TRUMPETER/HOBBY BOSS

Relative newcomers to the plastic modelling world, these companies are owned by the same corporation, are located at the same address and are essentially the same firm although different models are marketed separately under the two labels. Hobby Boss produces a 1/16 scale mid-production Tiger I while Trumpeter's range is far more extensive encompassing a number of 1/72 scale models and a 1/16 scale Tiger II which can be built with either the Production or earlier Porsche turret. There are also options of other late or early production features.

ACADEMY PLASTIC MODELS

Based in Korea, this company's Military Miniatures range of 1/35 scale figures and vehicles includes an early and mid production Tiger I, a late production version and a Hybrid model, not shown here, with later steel wheels, Zimmerit texture and early drum-style commander's cupola marketed as Tiger I Hybrid Gruppe Fehrmann referring to the six Tigers from Panzerschule 1 Bergen which were commanded by Oberleutnant Rudolf Fehrmann during the last days of the war. Like Tamiya, Academy kits are known for their striking, often action filled, box art.

Depicted at right is Academy's Tiger I mid-production kit No 1387 with interior detail and inset a view of the turret of the early version, model No 1348, also with interior detail.

HOBBY FAN/AFV CLUB

Hobby Fan Enterprises is the parent company of AFV Club, both of which are based in Taiwan. At the time of writing the AFV Club catalogue included a Sturmtiger, a Tiger I late production version, a Tiger I early production version and a Tiger I final production model, all in 1/35 scale. Most kits feature non-standard inclusions such as turned metal gun barrels, photo-etched brass parts and water-slide transfers offering numerous schemes. The company also provides accessories in the shape of both solid plastic and workable tracks for the Tiger I and Sturmtiger in both 1/35 and 1/48 scale in addition to ammunition, wooden crates and other general items. The 1/48 scale late production Tiger I model formally produced by Skybow is now marketed under the AFV Club logo.

Above : The AFV Club late production Tiger I in transport mode. This kit is essentially the same as their Tiger I Latest Model and the Tiger I late model Michael Wittmann Special with the inclusion, and omission, of selected parts.

ZVEZDA

Founded in 1990, this Russian company has grown from a backyard operation to become one of the country's larger exporters. The current catalogue features an early production Tiger in 1/35, a retooling of a 1996 kit. The same version is also offered in 1/72 and 1/100 scale. Their latest releases include a Tiger II with the Porsche turret and Zimmerit and a later Tiger II with the Production turret without Zimmerit, both reworkings of Dragon kits with new, added parts. A 1/72 scale Tiger II has been announced but had not been released at the time of writing and, judging by the rudimentary box art, may still be some way off.

Above: The currently available 1/35 scale Tiger kits from Zvezda. The company at one time offered a late production Tiger I which was apparently a re-boxing of the Italeri kit but this seems to be no longer in production. Below: The 1/72 scale early Tiger I and the Sturmtiger in 1/35 scale. The latter is a re-boxing on the Italeri kit originally released in 1997.

Above: Zvezda's early production Tiger I model number 3646 built from the box.

ITALERI

This Italian company has been producing plastic models since its foundation in 1962. At present the catalogue contains a Sturmtiger and Tiger I models depicting early, mid and late production versions in 1/35 scale. In 1/72 scale Italeri produces the Tiger II with the Production turret and a late production Tiger I in their Fast Assembly range, the latter kit containing two models comprising just ten pieces each. Of the large model manufacturers Italeri alone has ventured into 1/56 scale with a Tiger I late production kit. This scale complements 28mm wargames figures of which there are now quite a number on the market.

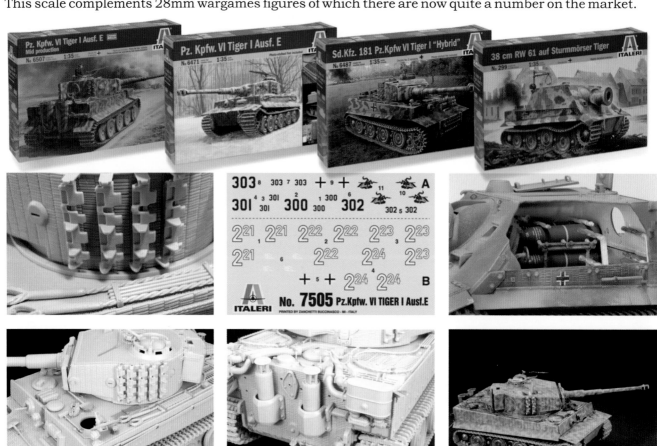

Above: Details of Italeri's late production Tiger I kit showing the spare track hangers and turret Zimmerit, the interior of the Strumtiger, the mid-production model with parts from Bren Gun of the Czech Republic and the 1/56 scale wargames model.

RYE FIELD MODELS

A relatively new model company based in Hong Kong, Rye Field Models has released three kits depicting Tiger I variants all in the short space of time between September 2015 and February 2016. Contrary to what has been written elsewhere these are not re-worked or re-issued kits but completely new models.

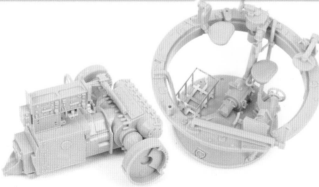

Rye Field's current catalogue includes an initial production model, specifically the Tigers that were sent to Tunisia, another early production model, slightly later than the Tunisian Tiger with interior detail and a late hybrid Tiger I with steel road wheels and early commander's cupola. It should be mentioned that these first two kits, as they are packaged, are not strictly relevant to the time period covered by this book including as they do parts that allow them to be built as vehicles which operated at specific times and in particular places and are really included here to complete our list. At left are some of the interior parts that are included with the sPz.Abt 503 Eastern Front Tiger I kit.

ROYAL MODEL

This Italian company has been producing high quality accessories and after market parts since the early 1990s under the guidance of its founder, Roberto Reale. The catalogue includes complete upgrade sets in 1/35 scale for the early, mid and late production Tiger I and for the Tiger II. Royal Model also market a limited number of sets in 1/72 and 1/48 scale and crew figures for the larger scale models.

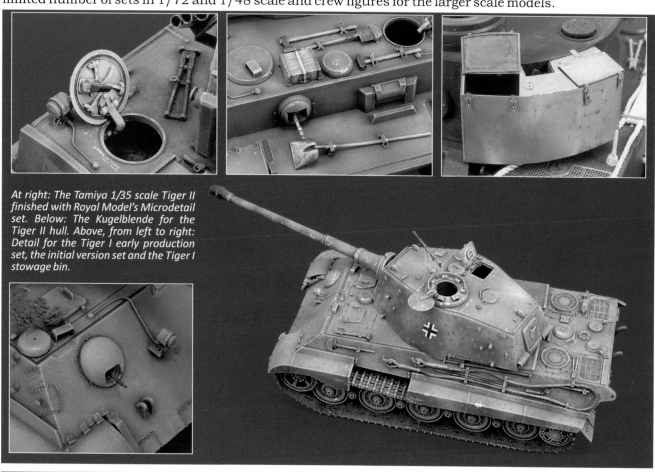

At right: The Tamiya 1/35 scale Tiger II finished with Royal Model's Microdetail set. Below: The Kugelblende for the Tiger II hull. Above, from left to right: Detail for the Tiger I early production set, the initial version set and the Tiger I stowage bin.

ROCHM MODEL

Rochm Model is the brainchild of modeller Sheng Hui whose work appears in the model showcase section of this book. Specialising in detail sets in resin, photo-etched brass and aluminium for the Tiger I, these products are really at the top end of the market. Modelmakers will be interested to know that Rochm Model is currently running a Tiger build competition with a first prize of a genuine Tiger track link.

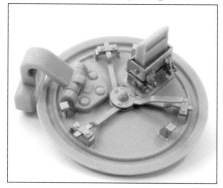

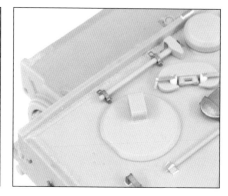

HAULER

Based in the Czech Republic, this company produces accessory sets in photo-etched brass and resin in 1/48, 1/35 and even 1/87 scale. A number of products are marketed under the Brengun logo and examples of these are depicted on page 52 under the heading for Italeri. The images shown above are all in 1/48 scale and show parts of the upgrade set for the AFV Club Sturmtiger, the photo-etched brass engine mesh covers for the Tamiya early production Tiger I and the exhaust covers and smaller details for the Tamiya Tiger II.

VOYAGER

Voyager have been manufacturing upgrade sets for scale models since 2003 with the release of their first set for 1/35 scale armour. The company also produces accessories in resin including Tiger I road wheels in transport mode. The sets shown above are 1.Dragon late production Tiger I. 2.Tamiya late production Tiger I. 3.Dragon Tiger II. 4.Trumpeter mid production Tiger I. 5.AFV Club Sturmtiger. 6.General mid production Tiger I.

At left: The Atak Model 'damaged' Zimmerit kit here applied to the Dragon 1/35 scale late production Tiger I. Atak Model from Poland produce accessory sets for armored vehicle models in 1/48, 1/35 and 1/16 scale. Manufactured for the most part in resin, the company specialises in supplying different patterns of Zimmerit and also conversion parts such as gun mantlets and exhaust fittings.

GRIFFON MODEL

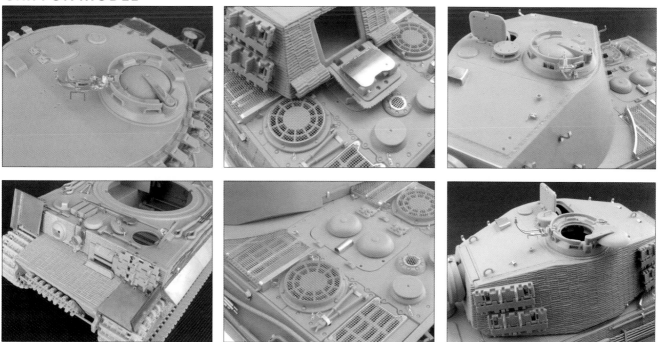

Based in China this company produces a large range of photo-etched brass sets for the Tiger I and Tiger II in 1/35 scale to fit most manufacturers kit, although they do recommend Tamiya and Dragon. Shown above are upgrade sets for the mid and late production Tiger I, the Tiger II Porsche turret and the Tiger II Series turret models.

ABER

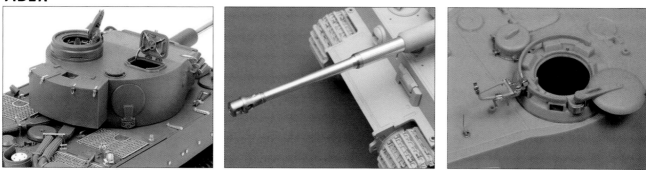

This Polish company has been manufacturing and selling upgrade sets since 1995 working in photo-etched brass, milled aluminium and brass, stainless steel and even wood. For some time now Tamiya has included a number of Aber products with their models. A full list of the accessories made specifically for the Tiger in all scales would be far too large to reproduce in this book comprehensively and the reader can find the company's contact details on page 64. The images shown above from left to right are part of the upgrade set for the Tamiya 1/16 scale early production Tiger I, which is actually made up from twelve smaller sets of photo-etched brass details, the barrel and muzzle brake suitable for either the mid or late production Tiger I in 1/35 scale made from brass and aluminium and parts of the upgrade set for the Tiger II Porsche turret, also in 1/35 scale.

E.T. MODELS

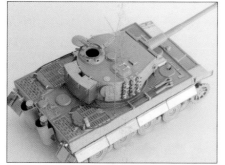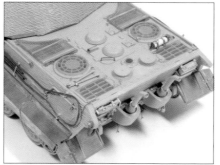

E.T. Models, a relatively new manufacturer from China, produce upgrade sets in 1/72 and 1/35 scale in brass and resin. Shown above, from left to right, are the etched-brass sets to fit the Dragon 1/72 scale late production Tiger I, the 1/35 scale set for the Dragon Tiger II Production turret kit and the Tiger I stowage box in 1/35 scale. Most sets are specifically designed, according to the company, to fit Dragon or Tamiya kits but some, for example the stowage bin, are referred to as universal.

FRIULMODEL

Based in Hungary, this company produces metal track sets for the Tiger I for the initial, early, mid, late production versions and transport tracks as well as the early and later variants for the Tiger II. Friulmodel also offer metal wheel sets for the Tiger II, both the early and later versions.

MODELKASTEN

This Japanese company produces injection moulded, plastic track sets in 1/35 scale. For the Tiger I Modelkasten offers a late model track set, a late model spare track set with white metal brackets, a transport track set and an early model track set which comes with white metal spare track brackets. These sets are all workable. For the Tiger II there is a non-workable track set, a fully workable track set, a spare track set, and a workable track set which includes fender stop brackets, a rotation adapter for the drive sprocket, an assembly tool and a number of spare links.

MODEL ARTISAN MORI

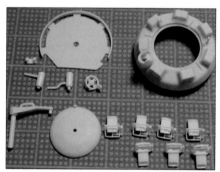

This small Japanese company produces resin upgrade parts for 1/35 scale armour models including detailed commander's cupolas for the Tiger I and Tiger II as well as more general items such as tool sets - including fire extinguishers, tow shackles and bolt cutters, a 20 ton jack and Bosch headlights in kit form.

RB MODEL

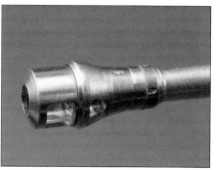

RB Model from Poland produce a range of milled aluminium and brass gun barrels and resin accessories for 1/35 scale armour models. Shown above, from left to right, are the 8.8cm KwK 36 L/56 for the early model Tiger I, the 8.8cm KwK 43/3 L/71 for the later model Tiger II and the 8.8cm KwK 36 L/56 gun for the later model Tiger I.

MODEL FACTORY HIRO

Although this Japanese company is best known for its multi-media racing car kits, they did venture into the world of armour modelling beginning in 2013 with the release of a limited edition rendering of an early production Tiger I followed within twelve months by a late production version, both in 1/35 scale. Both kits consist of parts made from resin, white metal and aluminium as well as photo-etched brass and a comprehensive sheet of water-slide transfers. Parts are included for interior details and the tracks and suspension are fully workable. At the time of writing the late production kit had been sold out and we have not been able to confirm rumours that the company may undertake another production run.

Above: Details from both the early and late production models. Below: The late production Tiger I from Model Factory Hiro's Ultimate Kit range shown here fully assembled with the exception of the mudguards and front fenders.

A late production Tiger I of 10.Kompanie, Panzer-Regiment Grossdeutschland photographed in Latvia during the summer of 1944. The vehiclel's number of B01 identifies this as the company commander's tank.

EQUIPMENT ALLOCATIONS AND LOSSES, III.ABTEILUNG, PANZER-REGIMENT GROSSDEUTSCHLAND, 1944

		Jan	Feb	Mar	Apr	May	Jun	Jul	Aug	Sep	Oct	Nov	Dec
Pz-Rgt GD	*Received*		10*	6	6	14**	12		12				4
Tiger I	*Lost*			5			2		10	7	18	2***	
	On Hand	13/6	13/10	14/10	20/8	28/13	38/26	38 (T)	40/19	33/11	15/8	13/12	17 (T)

*Allocated but did not arrive; ** 6 handed over to SS-Pz-Rgt 3; *** To sPz-Abt 502.

continued from page 16..

of the month. Badly depleted by the winter battles, the division spent the month of February refitting west of Kirovograd and in March moved to the area around Kishinev, present day Chisinau in Moldova, with just ten operational tanks.

In April the battalion, with the support of the division's Panzergrenadier-Regiment, conducted a successful attack between Targul Frumos and Jassy, modern Iasi in Romania, and took part in the counterattack and recapture of Bals. In May the Tigers were involved in the successful assault on both sides of Targul Frumos with the infantrymen from the division's Panzergrenadier-Regiment and Panzerfüsilier-Regiment and with elements of 3.SS-Panzer-Division on their left attacking along the road to Iasi. The month of June began with several small skirmishes until the second week when the division was moved to Bacua and remained there until the end of July. During this time six replacement Tigers, complete with crews taken from Panzer-Ersatz und Ausbildungs-Abteilung 500, were allocated to the battalion although two were destroyed by Soviet fighter-bombers as they are being unloaded at the front.

By the end of July the division had been moved to Gumbinnen in East Prussia. In August the division's Tigers were in action near Wirballen, now Virbalis in Lithuania, and in the attack to recapture Wilkowischken, now Vilkaviskis, subsequently withdrawing to Scaudvile. It was here that the battalion commander, Oberstleutnant Georg Baumunk, was severely wounded on 9 August when his tank, and two others of 10.Kompanie, were destroyed. By the end of the month the battalion was supporting Panzer-Brigade 104 and 1.Infanterie-Division in their attempts to capture Tukums, west of Riga in Latvia. During September the Tiger battalion with parts of 5.Panzer-Division including the Panthers of I.Abteilung, Panzer-Regiment 31, took part in Operation Cäsar a counterattack launched in response to the Soviet offensive aimed at capturing Riga. The attack was largely unsuccessful and by the end of September the battalion occupied defensive positions having lost seven tanks in the previous month.

On 9 October the division withdrew towards Memel and a number of tanks had to be destroyed for lack of fuel, while just one Tiger was knocked out by the Soviets and five tanks were lost to the bombs of the Luftwaffe. By the end of October the division began moving to East Prussia by sea with the first eight Tigers arriving in Pillau, modern Baltiysk, on 26 October. The battalion had lost eighteen tanks in the preceding month.

On 13 December the battalion was renamed schwere Panzer-Abteilung Grossdeutschland and in early January, with seventeen operational tanks, was redeployed to the front near Praschnitz, present day Przasnysz in Poland.

SS-PANZER-REGIMENT 1

Formed in late November 1942 as 4.Kompanie, SS-Panzer-Regiment 1, with personnel drawn from the regiment's own establishment, the new heavy company received ten Tigers and fifteen Pzkw III ausf J tanks on 21 January 1943. The company took part in the offensive to recapture Kharkov in February and March 1943 together with the Tigers of the Das Reich and Totenkopf divisions (1). On 22 April the three Waffen-SS companies were all upgraded to fourteen Tigers each and amalgamated to become schwere SS-Panzer-Abteilung under the direct command of 1.SS-Panzerkorps. In practice, however, the order was never implemented and all three companies remained with their parent divisions at the front (2). All three companies took part in the Kursk offensive losing just one tank each and at some time prior to this, exactly when is not known, the heavy company was renamed as 13.Kompanie, SS-Panzer-Regiment 1. On 28 July 1943 the complete division was hastily withdrawn from the front and ordered to Italy, handing over nine and eight Tigers to the heavy companies of the Das Reich and Totenkopf divisions respectively. Prior to this, on 19 July 1943, in what would appear to be a compromise between the 22 April directive and the wishes of the division commanders, an order was issued for the creation of a complete heavy battalion for I.SS-Panzerkorps comprising two new companies with the men of the old 13.Kompanie, SS-Panzer-Regiment 1 making up the battalion's third company.

EQUIPMENT ALLOCATIONS AND LOSSES, 13.KOMPANIE, SS-PANZER-REGIMENT 1, 1944

		Jan	Feb	Mar	Apr	May	Jun	Jul	Aug	Sep	Oct	Nov	Dec
SS-Pz-Rgt 1	Received			11									
Tiger I	Lost	7*	6**	5	6***								
	On Hand	6/4	0	6/3	0								

* Of 13 Tiger I on hand on 31 December 1943, 1 tank was lost on 1 January and 4 tanks were captured next day after breaking down. The 2 tanks received from depot maintenance on 12 January were apparently not counted in the total on hand although the 2 returned on 21 January were, giving the numbers shown here.
** Schneider states that 5 tanks were received on 29 February but I feel that they may not have been taken on hand until the following day. They were almost certainly the tanks promised on 10 February and actually issued three days later. The other 6 were possibly those issued by the Heereszeugamt on 11 January, the only allocation for that exact number before the regiment left Russia. Official records also indicate that 2 tanks were allocated on 14 January and a further 5 on 26 February although Schneider makes no direct mention of either, nor are the other sources any clearer. Further, 6 tanks issued to sPz-Abt 503 were originally intended for SS-Panzer-Regiment 1.
*** On 14 April the last tanks were handed to the workshops of LIX.Armeekorps and the last crews left for France.

Early production Tigers of 13.Kompanie, SS-Panzer-Regiment 1 photographed in late 1943 before they were covered with whitewash camouflage. The company's numbering system is explained on page 26 of the illustration section.

1.The three Waffen-SS divisions mentioned here were all classed as Panzergrenadier divisions until late 1943 when all were upgraded to Panzer divisions - 22 October for Leibstandarte Adolf Hitler and Das Reich and 22 November for the Totenkopf division. Although confusing, for the sake of accuracy, they are referred to here by the title that was appropriate when the action described took place.
2.The plan basically fell apart when the commander of 1.SS-Panzergrenadier-Division, SS-Obergruppenführer Dietrich, simply refused to relinquish any of his Tiger crews.

The division's service in Italy was limited to disarming units of the Italian army and it was not only possible to implement the order but also train the crews on their new tanks, twenty-seven of which arrived between 15 and 25 August 1943, including two command variants. On 22 October the battalion was officially renamed schwere SS-Panzer-Abteilung 101, however less than a week later on 28 October the two companies that had been provisionally organised were consolidated, once again named 13.Kompanie, and ordered back to Russia. The staff elements, including the battalion headquarters, most of the maintenance platoon, the headquarters company and the battalion's third company were moved to Truppenübungsplatz Senne in Germany. These units would continue their training as schwere SS-Panzer-Abteilung 101, first in Germany and then at Maisieres in Belgium, while 13.Kompanie was engaged in the east arriving in Berdychiv, south of Zhitomir in what is today western Ukraine, on 12 November 1943. During the remainder of the year 13.Kompanie took part in the defensive battles west of Kiev and on the last day of 1943 the company reported that just two tanks were combat ready.

On 1 January all the tanks that had returned to the front were undergoing repairs at Pjatki near Trajanov and during the subsequent withdrawal to Starokostiantyniv, 35 kilometres north of Khmelnytskyi, four of those were lost bringing the company's total to just nine. By 12 January, however, enough tanks were combat ready to take part in a counterattack near Zherebky and in the following days cut off and destroyed an enemy breakthrough. On 1 March, 13.Kompanie was officially deactivated and the crews began moving to Belgium to join schwere SS-Panzer-Abteilung 101. On 5 March, however, six new Tigers arrived and these were manned by the tank crews that had not yet left for the west and integrated into a battle group with the remainder of the Panzer regiment as Panzergruppe SS-Panzer-Division Leibstandarte Adolf Hitler. Within days these tanks were in action, supported by schwere Panzer-Abteilung 503, as part of Kampfgruppe Kulmann, in an attack to open the highway to Manachyn, moving as far east as Solomna on the Sataniv - Viitivtsi road and linking up with elements of 7.Panzer-Division.

In early April, with just three operational tanks, the Panzergruppe had reached Buchach on the Strypa River near Ternopil and were operating with 10.SS-Panzer-Division Frundsberg. On 14 April all tanks were handed over to the maintenance units of LIX.Armeekorps and within two days the last of the Tiger crews left for the west.

After fighting in Normandy and the Ardennes, schwere SS-Panzer-Abteilung 101 returned to the eastern Front in February 1945.

SS-PANZER-REGIMENT 2 DAS REICH

Created at the same time as the heavy company of SS-Panzer-Regiment 1 this unit's formation began in early December 1942 at Fallingbostel while a number of crews were trained at the Henschel works in Kassel.

In December 1942 the company received its first Tigers and at some time before the unit left for the front in late January 1943 it was named 8.Kompanie, SS-Panzer-Regiment 2. The company took part in the recapture of Kharkov and in Operation Citadel after which just five Tigers were considered as ready for operations, although just one was destroyed. During August 1943 the company fought in the defensive battles along the Mius river and again around the city of Kharkov which was lost for the last time on 22 August 1943.

In November the company was involved in the defensive battles around Kiev and it was at this time that Hauptscharführer Hans Soretz claimed to have knocked out the 2,000th Russian tank destroyed by the regiment. In December 1943 most of the division was withdrawn from the front and moved to France, leaving behind a small battle group named SS-Panzergruppe Das Reich which included five Tigers, four Pzkw V Panthers and five Pzkw IV tanks - the last of the Panzer regiment.

Said to have been photographed on 1 December 1943 near Zhitomir, these Tigers are operating with Panzergruppe Das Reich, also referred to as Kampfgruppe Lammerding. The tank in the image at left and in the foreground at right is Tiger S33 while the other vehicle has been identified as Tiger S13. If the date is correct these tanks are two of just three combat ready Tigers that 8.Kompanie had available. Note that S33, and probably S13, still has its Kursk markings.

EQUIPMENT ALLOCATIONS AND LOSSES, 8.KOMPANIE, SS-PANZER-REGIMENT 2, 1944

		Jan	Feb	Mar	Apr	May	Jun	Jul	Aug	Sep	Oct	Nov	Dec
SS-Pz-Rgt 2	Received		5**										
Tiger I	Lost			5***									
	On Hand	0*	5/5	0									
	** The last tanks were lost on Christmas Day 1943. ** The 5 tanks received on 5 February had taken over three weeks*												
	to reach the front having been dispatched on 17 January												
	**** 3 tanks were lost on a single day, 3 March, when 1 was captured, 1 destroyed by enemy action and 1 by its own*												
	crew. On 24 March Tiger number 01 was lost and the last Tiger, number 02, fought on until 26 March despite												
	crashing through a bridge and surviving a fall of four metres just five days previously. Both were destroyed by												
	their own crews.												

On Christmas Day 1943 the last three serviceable tanks were abandoned at the crossing of the Teteriv river near Radomyshl in northern Ukraine, some due to a lack of fuel. This left the Panzergruppe with just the two Tigers which had earlier been sent to the maintenance depots and on 29 December a number of men were despatched to Germany to pick up five new tanks which would not arrive until the following February. When the new tanks arrived they were immediately thrown into the fighting to support elements of 19.Panzer-Division around Shepetivka in western Ukraine and the counterattack against the Horyn bridgehead at Hulivtsi.

On 8 March 1944 what remained of the division was incorporated into SS-Regimentsgruppe Das Reich with the surviving armoured vehicles - including two Tigers, numbered 01 and 02 - consolidated into a mixed tank company of four platoons (1). On Friday, 24 March Tiger 01 was destroyed by its crew as was Tiger 02 on the following Sunday. The surviving tank crews remained with SS-Regimentsgruppe Das Reich until 14 April when the division was transported to France. In April 1943, when the original order to create a heavy tank battalion for I.SS-Panzerkorps was issued, 2.SS-Panzergrenadier-Division had supplied 120 men who eventually arrived at Senne in the following month to begin their training. In July they were transferred to the Eastern Front and attached to the Das Reich division with a view to continuing their training in an operational environment although a number of crews found themselves fighting as infantry.

In October all were returned to Germany where, on 4 November 1943, the battalion received its official title of schwere SS-Panzer-Abteilung 102 (2). The battalion completed its training at Wezep in Holland, the last crews receiving their tanks on the very day the Allies landed in Normandy, and remained in the west until early 1945.

SS-PANZER-REGIMENT 3 TOTENKOPF

Formed as 9.Kompanie, SS-Panzer-Regiment 3 at the same time as the heavy companies of the other Waffen-SS divisions. The tank crews were drafted from replacement personnel of SS-Panzer-Regiment 1 and SS-Panzer-Regiment 2 with some men from the reconnaissance platoons and the first and second battalions of SS-Panzer-Regiment 3. The first Tigers were received during January 1943 and by 10 February the company was ordered to the Russian Front.

The company went into action for the first time on 21 February 1943 near Pavlograd on the Samara river in eastern Ukraine, attacking through an intense snowstorm. The company supported operations by the Adolf Hitler and Das Reich divisions until 17 February when it was reunited with its parent formation. The Totenkopf division was continuously active throughout the remainder of 1943 taking part in Operation Citadel, including the battle at Prokhorovka, and the attempts to defend Kharkov.

In January 1944, tanks of SS-Panzer-Regiment 3 - including three Tigers, five Pzkw III and ten Pzkw IV tanks - were attached to Kampfgruppe Gusovius at Inhulo-Kamyanka, south-east of Kirovograd for a counterattack to recapture Nikolajewka (3). The attack punched through two Soviet anti-tank belts but could not penetrate the third and the Tigers were withdrawn to Bobrynets south of Kirovograd.

The heavy tanks were able to rest during most of February due to the rains and the muddy conditions that followed. In early March, during an attack aimed at Novoukrainka, south-west of Kirovograd the company commander, SS-Obersturmführer Baetke, was killed. For the remainder of March the Tigers were employed singly over the whole front covering the withdrawal across the Dniester at Dubossary, modern Dubasari in Moldova, territory which in 1944 was part of Romania.

On 14 April the last serviceable tanks had managed to reach Tiraspol and Balti, approximately 45 kilometres to the south, only to learn that all railway traffic had been halted. Consequently the last Tigers were destroyed by their crews and the division moved to Bacua in Romania a further 80 kilometres to the west. On 2 May three new Tigers arrived and these were sent into action immediately in an attack south of Pietriscu and north towards Helestieni near the current Moldova-Romanian border.

After this assault the company settled into defensive positions around Raginoasa, near Pascani. By the end of the month the division's available tanks - plus a

---

1. These Tigers were the tanks that were mentioned as being in repair in December 1943.
2. Although the order was dated 22 October 1943 it was apparently not put into effect until the date shown here.
3. I have been unable to locate Nikolajewka on any map, contemporary or modern, however if the documents used to create Schneider's account are correct the Russian anti-tank positions may well have been to the south of Adzhamka placing Nikolajewka somewhere along the Kirovograd-Oleksandriya road. Kampfgruppe Gusovius was made up primarily from units of 13.Panzer-Division.

Above: Photographed in Poland in summer 1944 this turret is from a late production Tiger I of the ninth company's first platoon. The single aperture for the monocular gun sight introduced in March 1944 and lack of sockets for the jib boom indicate that this is one of the seven Tigers received in May 1944. Note that the metal ring for the anti-aircraft machine gun has been removed although the bracket for the gun seems to have been retained. The high contrast between the colour of the spare tracks and the turret is obvious here. German tank tracks were made from an alloy of steel and manganese and were painted before they left the factory and surviving examples can be found in red oxide primer and a very dark, almost black shade.

further two Tigers handed over from Panzer-Regiment Grossdeutschland - had been hastily formed into a Panzergruppe and positioned north-east of Targul Frumos as a rapid reaction force. During June the Tigers, including six new tanks that had been picked up from Magdeburg in early May, supported SS-Panzergrenadier-Regiment 5 Thule in the relief of Kampfgruppe Knobelsdorf encircled in Podu Iloaiei, east of Targul Frumos on the road to Iasi.

The Tigers of 9.Kompanie were briefly attached to 24.Panzer-Division but by the end of June the company had returned to Bacau.

In early July 1944 the division moved to Brest, in western Belarus, to counter the Russian offensive and were immediately sent north for the defence of Grodno. On 18 July the Tigers moved into defensive positions in front of Sapotskin in the Neman bridgehead to the north of the city. On the same day the new company commander, SS-Hauptsturmführer Fischer, was killed when his Tiger was hit by anti-tank fire which may have come from the neighbouring 4.SS-Polizei-Panzergrenadier-Division. On the following day Sapotskin was taken and soon after the division was moved to Siedlice, 60 kilometres to the east of Warsaw, to counter a possible Soviet breakthrough on the Vistula.

On the last day of July, SS-Hauptscharführer Berger with several tank crews was sent into Warsaw to pick up five repaired Tigers which had been delivered to the Warszawa-Praga railway station on the eastern bank of the Vistula. From the station the tanks were ordered to drive to the SS-Stauferkaserne on Rakowiecka Street near the corner of Kazimierzowska Street where a replacement battalion of the division was stationed. There are several conflicting accounts of the actions, and even the numbers of 9.Kompanie Tigers involved in the fighting in the Warsaw Uprising (1). What is certain is that as late as 12 August 1944, 9.Armee reported that six Tigers were on hand in Warsaw and that two had been lost in the fighting.

During August and September the division was engaged east of Radzymin near the Narev river where the company commander, SS-Obersturmführer Neidhardt, was killed when he ventured outside his tank on a reconnaissance. The Tigers supported SS-Panzergrenadier-Regiment 6 Theodor Eicke and SS-Panzerjäger-Abteilung 3 in counterattacks near the village of Josefow, west of Radzymin, and an attack on Rembelszczyzna, on the road to Legionowo between the Narev and Vistula rivers, which was ultimately unsuccessful. In the following month however the company managed to push the Russians back to Josefow and took up defensive positions.

Most of November and December were spent in maintenance and resupply and by Christmas Eve the division began moving to Hungary reaching Komorn west of Budapest on 29 December.

On the last day of 1944 the company received orders to prepare for an attack along the Nyergesujfalu road to Budapest the next day. The tanks all received a coat of whitewash and that night the crews welcomed in the new year with a party.

1.The most detailed English language account of the company's actions in Warsaw is quite contradictory from the beginning, stating for example that on 1 August Berger's Tigers crossed the Poniatowski bridge heading east and moved along Pankiewcza Street and Marszalkowska Street to the corner of Koszilkowa Street, all of which are in fact on the west bank of the Vistula near the Stauferkaserne. It is possible that the five Tigers under Berger's command were already under repair at the Stauferkaserne and that the tanks delivered to the Praga station on 31 July were in fact the five new tanks sent from Heereszeugamt Magdeburg on 26 July and forwarded on from Lochow. A total figure of ten and the subsequent destruction of two, with the three that Schneider says returned to the company on 2 August and the single Tiger that returned from the maintenance depot at Osowiec on 7 August would at least agree with the 9.Armee total.

EQUIPMENT ALLOCATIONS AND LOSSES, 9.KOMPANIE, SS-PANZER-REGIMENT 3, 1944

		Jan	Feb	Mar	Apr	May	Jun	Jul	Aug	Sep	Oct	Nov	Dec
SS-Pz-Rgt 3	*Received*					7***	8****	10					
Tiger I	*Lost*	7			9**			2	4	1			
	On Hand	9/4*	9/4	9 (T)	0	7 (T)	15/9	23	19	18/6	18/6	18/10	18/11
	* On 1 January 1944 the company had 16 tanks in total with 2 ready for operations. ** This figure is based on the claim - certainly true - that all remaining tanks were destroyed on this day and the lack of reports of any vehicles destroyed in the preceeding two months although 2 were seriously damaged. *** 3 Tigers were picked up from Magdeburg in Germany by their crews and returned on 2 May. On 20 May 4 tanks, 2 new vehicles and 2 veterans, were handed over from Panzer-Regiment Grossdeutschland. **** 6 of these tanks were diverted from s.SS-Pz-Abt 103 which was training in Germany at the time.												

This unit should not be confused with schwere SS-Panzer-Abteilung 103 which was established as a heavy tank battalion for III.(Germanisches) SS-Panzerkorps in November 1943. This battalion's personnel were drawn from replacements who were originally intended for a proposed second battalion for SS-Panzer-Abteilung 11 Hermann von Salza which was to be upgraded to a regiment. The battalion's formation was constantly delayed when men and vehicles were siphoned off to replace losses in the other Waffen-SS Tiger units including the battalion's first six tanks which were handed over to 9.Kompanie, SS-Panzer-Regiment 3. The battalion was sent to the Eastern Front in January 1945 and first saw action near Küstrin where some of the Tiger crews were, quite literally, fighting for their own homes.

Below: Mid production Tiger number 902 of SS-Panzer-Regiment 3 photographed in late 1943. This tank was built after August 1943 when the single headlight became standard and prior to October when the S-Mine dischargers were dropped from production. The solid black turret numbers lasted until the first snow fell in early December and the tanks were coated with whitewash. After this small boards marked with the tank's number were suspended from the turret until spring 1944 when the system of white outline numbers was introduced.

As with most major weapons systems, the Tiger was subject to an extensive series of modifications in an effort to increase its effectiveness and to remedy problems that had arisen during trials or actual combat. The modifications listed here are those carried out during production and generally do not concern the many additions and ad-hoc solutions made by units in the field, some of which are shown and discussed in the illustration section. As the purpose of this chapter is to supply sufficient information for the reader to accurately and confidently determine when a particular tank was manufactured, the many internal changes are for the most part not listed. In addition technical details of the prototypes and earliest versions, often referred to today as initial production models, fall outside the time frame of this study and are also not included. These may be covered in a future title.

The Tiger I chassis was assembled by the firm of Henschel und Sohn at their huge plant at Kassel, conveniently located just 50 kilometres from the Paderborn-Sennelager training grounds. Each chassis was given a unique number or Fahrgestellnummer (Fgst), the series beginning with 250001. The turrets were manufactured by Wegmann & Co., also located in Kassel, and shipped to Henschel where the final assembly took place. Each turret could also be identified by a number, here referred to as a Turm Nr. Although the official designation changed during this time the term Tiger I is used here, and in other parts of this book, as a matter of convenience.

Tiger I, early production model completed May 1943. This tank features the periscope for the loader and its armoured cover on the turret roof, the new drive sprocket which was machined flat, the dischargers for the smoke candles or Nebelwurfgeräte on the turret side and the S-Mine dischargers on the hull introduced from August 1942 and January 1943 respectively, the spare tracks

and their brackets on the hull side and the modified Fiefel air cleaning system. Not visible on our drawing is the reinforced gun mantlet introduced as early as November 1942, the triangular access port on the rear deck, the cast louvres on the hull rear deck, which from April 1943 were both identical, and the second hole in the starter alignment plate introduced with the HL 230 P45 engine.

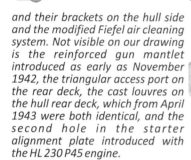

1. The early drum-style cupola replaced in June 1943. 2. The modified gun mantlet showing the vertical, armoured reinforcement around the gun sight apertures. 3. The starter alignment plate, pictured here on the hull rear between the exhaust outlets. The second, offset hole was introduced with the Maybach HL 230 P45 engine in May 1943.

March 1943. A fixed loader's periscope, protected by an armoured cover, was installed on the turret roof beginning with Turm Nr.184. Modified Fiefel air filters were introduced and the cap over the ventilation riser on the rear deck was replaced by a triangular-shaped opening covered by a flat plate held in place by three bolts.

April 1943. From Fgst Nr.251205 the hub of the drive sprocket was machined flat to allow the bolts with their reinforced tabs to be better secured. Beginning in mid-April three spare track links were mounted on the turret right side between the vision port and the escape hatch and five spare track links on the left side between the vision slit and the pistol port. In late April the links on the right side were reduced to two. Interestingly it was initially planned

to fix fifteen spare links around the hull sides but the introduction of the stowage bin meant this was no longer possible.

May 1943. A second hole in the alignment plate on the hull rear was introduced with the Maybach HL 230 P45 engine.

June 1943. Beginning with Turm Nr.286 the smoke candle dischargers, or Nebelwurfgeräte, were deleted. These had first been added in August 1942.

July 1943. From Turm Nr.391 on Fgst. Nr.250391 a redesigned turret was introduced. Its most obvious feature was the commander's cupola made from a cast armoured ring fitted with seven periscopes, each with an armoured cover, and a hatch with a pivoting arm. On the first few cupolas, perhaps as

Tiger I, mid production model completed October 1943. The most striking difference is the new turret with simplified turret ring and cast cupola. The large pistol port on the turret side has been replaced by a plug and the modified turret vision ports have a wider slit and lower profile. The loader's periscope has a wider armour guard. The smoke candle and S-Mine dischargers have been deleted and a single headlight is now mounted

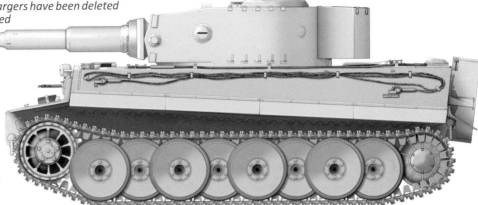

at the centre of the hull front plate. The ventilation fan has been moved from the rear of the turret roof to a point directly over the centre of the gun breech. Not visible on our drawing are the Gleitschulzpickeln tracks and the starter crank handle which is now stowed by the antenna base. The edges of the escape hatch on the right side of the turret are no longer beveled.

1.The June 1943 cast commander's cupola. Note also the spare tracks, the brackets holding them to the turret and the cast engine louvres . 2.The forward opening hatch fitted to some of the first mid production tanks. 3.The Gleitschutzpickeln tracks with metal chevrons first issued in October 1943.

many as thirty, the hatch swung towards the front and was later redesigned to open towards the rear. A partial ring, welded to the tops of the periscope guards, acted as a track for the anti-aircraft machine gun mount. A new loader's periscope was installed with a wider armoured cover and the loader's hatch was given a modified lock which could be adjusted from the outside. The exhaust fan on the turret roof was provided with a new armoured guard and moved from the rear of the turret roof to a position in front of the cupola directly above the gun breech. The large pistol port on the left turret rear was replaced by a simple plug. The fasteners for the track replacement cable were moved to new positions along the hull left side and a single headlight was placed at the top left corner of the hull front replacing the two headlights mounted at each corner. The edges of the turret escape hatch which had been beveled to follow the contour of the turret sides were left flat.

August 1943. To simplify production all deep wading components were dropped. The vision slits on the turret sides were redesigned with a wider slit allowing for better all round vision and with a lower profile. Beginning with Fgst Nr.250461 redesigned fasteners to hold the track replacement cable were welded to the hull side. A thick paste commercially known as Zimmerite - better known today as Zimmerit - was applied to all vertical surfaces that could be reached by a man of average height. Ridges were worked into the paste, the intention being to prevent magnetic mines gaining a hold. There is some debate about the date of introduction with July and September also being given.

September 1943. Beginning with Fgst Nr.250496, large hooks, sometimes referred to as a 'C' clamps were mounted on the rear hull to the left of the exhaust guard and on the hull deck to the right of the driver's hatch.

October 1943. Tracks with Gleitschutzpickeln, or metal chevrons, were introduced from Fgst Nr.250570. These were intended to be used for cross country running in order to preserve road surfaces. The Feifel air filters, together with the brackets for the hoses and ductwork, were discontinued. The five S-Mine dischargers on the hull, four in the case of command tanks, were dropped from production. The outer disc on the loader's hatch was discontinued. Beginning with Fgst Nr. 250570 the crank handle was moved to a position near the antenna. The track tool box on the left hull rear plate was discontinued.

November 1943. Beginning with Fgst Nr.250635 and ending with Fgst Nr.250875, an external travel lock for the main gun was installed on the rear hull at the right corner. During November eighteen Panzerbefelswagen command tanks were converted by having the base for the Sternantenne covered by a metal plate and the aperture for the turret roof antenna plugged. The antenna base on the left side of the hull deck was retained and used for the Fu.5 radio.

December 1943. The single headlight was moved to the centre of the front plate. The mounts for the Feifel air filters are no longer attached.

January 1944. A 20ton jack with new mount replaced the 15ton model from Fgst Nr.250772. The fasteners and shovel on the glacis were dropped from production as was the turret pistol plug. Hull extensions at the front were notched to allow freer movement of the towing shackles and the hull extensions at the rear were also reshaped.

February 1944. Rubber-cushioned, steel-tired road wheels were introduced beginning with Fgst Nr 250822. The number of road wheels on each axle was decreased from three to two meaning that it was no longer necessary to remove the outer wheels for rail travel. At the same time a smaller diameter idler was introduced. An access port for the blowtorch with an oval shaped armoured cover was created on the tail plate below the armoured guard for the left muffler. A turret ring guard was welded to the deck beginning with Fgst Nr 250850 necessitating a rearranging of the tool stowage on the hull deck. From Fgst Nr. 250876 the external travel lock for the main gun was on longer installed. From Fgst Nr.250875 a new U-shaped tow shackle was issued.

March 1944. A new turret roof was installed from Fgst Nr. 250991. These were 40mm thick and at first were constructed from a single piece of armour plate, bent to slope downwards at the front. From May 1944 the roof was made up of two pieces welded at the join directly behind the armour cover for the loader's periscope. The loader's hatch originally designed for the Tiger II was installed. This was

countersunk into the new armoured roof and the protective frame was dropped from production. The Nahverteidigungswaffe close defence weapon, authorised in January, was installed

April 1944. The T.Z.F.9c monocular gun sight replaced the T.Z.F.9b binocular version. As a number of gun mantlets had been manufactured with two apertures before the order was received, the outermost was sealed with an armoured plug and welded shut. As the tanks were subsequently covered with Zimmerit, these plugs are almost impossible to discern in contemporary photographs. In an attempt at standardisation the 8.8cm KwK36 L/56 guns of a number of tanks were fitted with a light weight muzzle brake designed for the 8.8cm KwK43 L/71 of the Tiger II.

May 1944. A wider track pin return plate was mounted on both sides of the hull above the idlers. Drainage slits were cut into the cast commander's cupola

June 1944. Three sockets were welded to the turret roof to support a 2ton jib boom. This modification was ordered to be retrofitted to older models. From Fgst Nr.2521205 double locking strips, shared by two nuts, were introduced on the track tooth ring of the drive sprocket. This was made necessary by the differences in casting which did not always result in centred locations for securing the nuts.

Tiger I, late production model completed June 1944. These late production tanks can be easily identified by the steel-tired road wheels and notched hull extensions. Also shown here is the two-piece 40mm turret roof, the sockets for The 2ton jib boom, the light weight muzzle brake

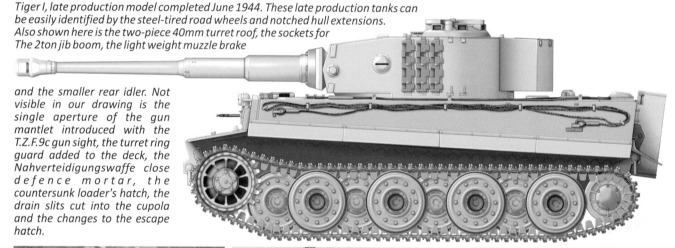

and the smaller rear idler. Not visible in our drawing is the single aperture of the gun mantlet introduced with the T.Z.F.9c gun sight, the turret ring guard added to the deck, the Nahverteidigungswaffe close defence mortar, the countersunk loader's hatch, the drain slits cut into the cupola and the changes to the escape hatch.

1.Nearest to the camera is one of the sockets for the jib boom and at right, in front of the loaders hatch, is the Nahverteidigungswaffe. 2.The single headlight and aperture for the monocular gun sight. 3.The turret ring guard introduced in February 1944 is just visible behind and below the gun mantlet.

In July and August 1944 the last fifty-four Tiger I tanks, numbered as Fgst Nr.251293 to Fgst Nr.251346, were assembled using thirty-two turrets which had been returned from combat units for major rebuilds and twenty-two new turrets. Modifications that were deemed necessary were the complete replacement of the turret roof with a 40mm thick armour plate, the installation of a cast cupola ring welded to the turret roof, the holes for the older style pistol port or the plug were covered and the new loader's hatch installed. Any other changes would need to be carried out at the assembly plants. In June 1944 the possibility of installing poison gas detection equipment on the Tiger I was discussed and although it is unknown if this progressed past the planning stage the manufacture of turrets continued well into August and as this modification was introduced on the Tiger II in July, it is therefore possible that poison gas detection panels were installed on the very last Tiger I tanks.

Although the designation Tiger II would suggest that this vehicle was a development of the Tiger I, it was in fact a completely new tank owing more to the Panther than it did to its predecessor. Indeed, it was envisaged that many components of the new Tiger would be compatible with the proposed Panther II. Both Porsche and Henschel competed for the design with Henschel's submission for the hull and suspension being finally accepted for production. The firm of Krupp had originally been contracted to build the turrets for the Porsche hull. However, on 17 February 1943, it was decided that production would cease after the final assembly of the fifty turrets that were either finished or in an advanced stage of completion. Concerns had been raised over the possibility of the curved turret front acting as a shot trap, deflecting anti-tank rounds downwards through the roof of the hull, but this was not the sole reason with the complexity of construction and the inadequacy of the frontal armour also being cited. The Henschel turret, which had been developed at the same time was accepted for production as the Serien-Turm or series turret, sometimes referred to as the Produktions Turm. The actual manufacture of the series turret was undertaken by Wegmann while the final assembly was completed at Henschel's Kassel plant. It was decided that the fifty completed Krupp turrets be utilised as an interim measure and all were handed over to Wegmann where Henschel components such as the elevation gear were installed. These were then each fitted to a standard chassis at Kassel. As they were originally intended for the Porsche chassis, which was never put into production, the Krupp turrets are often erroneously referred to today as the Porsche Turm. In spite of the significant difference in silhouette, the roofs of both the Krupp and Henschel turrets were laid out in the same manner with the cast commander's cupola, fume extractor, Nahverteidigungswaffe close defence weapon and loader's hatch placed centrally, the loader's periscope with its armoured cover towards the front and a shell ejection port towards the rear. Both had an escape hatch on the turret rear plate. As with the Tiger I a number of modifications were carried out before production ceased in March 1945 and the most important are listed here. Although more correctly referred to as Pzkw VI Tiger ausf B, the name Tiger II is used here.

Tiger II, completed January 1944. The first production tank has the standard curved track guards, tool stowage,

sheet metal covers for the exhausts and 40mm armour plate added to the turret roof. Of special note is the armoured cover over the opening for the deep-wading equipment, the eighteen-tooth drive sprocket and the lack of a turret guard ring. The view port, or Schauloch, next to the pistol port was welded shut. The coating of Zimmerit, which this tank certainly had, has been omitted for clarity.

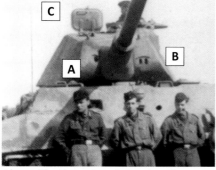

Above: The Krupp turret showing the aperture for the machine gun (A) and the binocular gun sight (B). Also shown is the loader's hatch in the open position (C). Note that this tank does not have the cut out in front of the radio operator's periscope. The hull rear plate with the early hull extensions with towing shackle (D), the sheet metal exhaust covers (E) and the jack (F). The roof of a damaged Krupp turret looking forward with the partly opened shell ejection port (G) and the Nahverteidigungswaffe close defence weapon (H).

January 1944. From Fgst Nr.280001, the first production Tiger II, the flat front fenders were replaced by a curved version with fixed sideplates. A coat of Zimmerit anti-magnetic mine paste was applied from the start of production.

February 1944. Curved exhaust pipes were fitted in place of the upright models and the metal shield for the exhausts was dropped from production. An access port with an armoured cover for the blowtorch was added on the rear plate below the left exhaust.

April 1944. A notch was cut from the edge of the glacis in front of the radio operator's periscope to allow a better field of view. The hull front extensions were modified to allow for the carrying of C hooks and the hull extensions at the rear were modified to

allow the hooks to pivot upwards. A turret ring guard was added to the hull for tanks with the Krupp turret. The T.Z.F 9b/1 binocular gunsight was replaced by the T.Z.F.9d monocular model. With this change a new gun mantlet was introduced with a single aperture for the gunsight and the redundant apertures of the Krupp turrets were plugged and welded shut. A new two-piece gun tube was introduced to replace the original monobloc version of the Kwk 43 L/71 gun. A lighter muzzle brake was also introduced.

May 1944. A new double link track, designated Gg 26/800/300 replaced the Gelandekette Gg 24/800/300 design fitted to the first vehicles. These tracks were also back fitted to older tanks. The drive sprocket for the new tracks had nine teeth in place of

Tiger II, completed June 1944. This tank has the sockets welded to the turret roof, the commander's blade sight, the two-piece gun tube, the turret ring guard, the nine-tooth drive sprocket introduced with the Gg 26/800/300

tracks and the curved exhaust pipes. The armoured cover for the deep-wading equipment has been deleted as has the metal guards for the engine exhausts. Not visible in our drawing is the notch in the glacis in front of the driver's periscope, the single aperture for the monocular gun sight and the vent on the rear deck for the fuel system. This tank would also have been coated in Zimmerit.

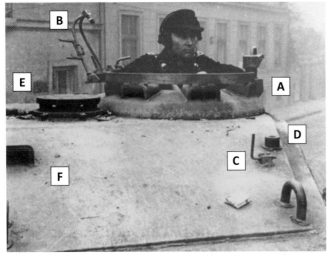

Above: The cast commander's cupola (A) complete with anti-aircraft machine gun mount (B). The two wires welded to the front periscope are clearly visible here as is the blade sight (C) in front of the boom socket(D). To the left of the cupola is the armoured cover for the extractor fan (E) and partially visible is the cover for the loader's periscope (F). Note that the cupola hatch has been removed. The photograph at right depicts the same tank and shows the monocular gun sight (G) and the poison gas panel bracket welded to the gun mantlet (H).

the previous eighteen. A blade sight for the commander was mounted on the turret roof at the left front corner. This was lined up with two wires welded over the foremost periscope of the cupola.

June 1944. The hinged armoured cover for the deep wading equipment was deleted and replaced by a heavy wire mesh screen. This modification had in fact been carried out on most production Tigers but became standard in June. Three sockets were welded to the turret roof to hold the 2ton jib boom and these were also retrofitted to older models. From Fgst Nr.280048 a number of turrets designed by Krupp with strengthened, sloping frontplate and without the bulge for the commander's cupola were adapted for use with the Henschel chassis.

A new, 40 mm thick loader's hatch was introduced.

July 1944. Hangers and fasteners were welded to both sides of the turret to hold double lengths of spare track. Brackets for poison gas identification panels were welded to the top of the gun mantlet and the turret roof at the right rear corner.

August 1944. Between April and August three additional Krupp designed turrets were completed and fitted to Henschel chassis. Narrower transport tracks were carried on the Ssyms-80ton railway wagon and to distinguish these tracks from those used for the Tiger I, two or three links out of every ten were supposed to have been painted red. A redesigned commander's cupola was introduced, mounted in a machined recess and secured by

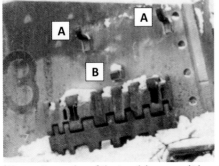

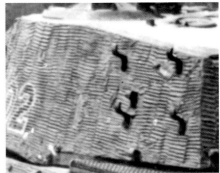

Above: Examples of the track hangers (A) and fasteners (B) fitted to both sides of the turret from July 1944. The detailed instructions and drawings issued in November, when these were retrofitted to older tanks, show that a track pin was supposed to hold the lower link to the fastener.

Above, left: The narrow tracks issued for rail travel in August 1944 and the nine-tooth drive sprocket which replaced the earlier eighteen-tooth version during production in May 1944. At right: The rear idler and early Gg 24/800/300 cross country tracks.

Tiger II, completed September 1944. This tank has the Serien-Turm or series turret introduced in June 1944 with hangers and fasteners for spare track links and brackets for poison gas

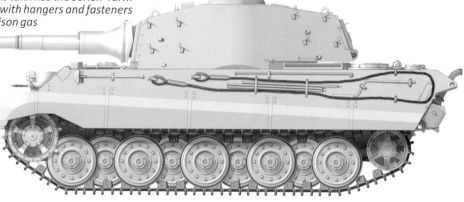

identification panels fixed to the gun mantlet and behind the lifting eye on the turret roof at the rear. From August the commander's cupola was bolted to the turret roof. Not visible in our drawing are the armour guards for the torsion bars on turret rear, the armoured cover over the engine compartment on the rear deck and the 40mm thick loader's hatch introduced in June 1944.

seven bolts. On 19 August 1944 an army order was issued directing that tanks were now to be painted in a standardised colour scheme before leaving the assembly plant. Large patches of Olivgrün RAL 6003 and Rotbraun RAL 8017 were to be applied over the Dunkelgelb RAL 7028 base colour. Photographic evidence shows that the edges varied from slightly feathered to a high-contrast, sharp line. In what may have been one variation of this basic pattern, each colour or patch also contained small dots of an alternate colour. This scheme, generally known today as Ambush camouflage, is shown in the illustration section. Every effort was made to deliver the remaining August consignment in the factory applied camouflage although the number can have been no more than ninety-four, the complete production for the month with sixty-three tanks leaving the factory in September and a further twenty-six in October by which time new painting instructions were issued. From Fgst Nr.280177 the interiors were no longer painted in Elfenbein RAL 1001, a very light, ivory shade, but left in their coat of Rot RAL 8012, a red oxide primer.

September 1944. An order of 9 September directed that the application of Zimmerit was to cease immediately.

October 1944. An order of 31 October stipulated that Henschel was to cease the use of Dunkelgelb RAL 7028 as a base colour for armoured vehicles. Tanks were from now on the be painted in a camouflage scheme made up of patches of Olivgrün, Rotbraun and Dunkelgelb over the basic red oxide primer. Curiously the order went on to state that if

Dunkelgelb was not available, Dunkelgrau RAL 7021 was a permissible alternative although these two colours are at almost opposite ends of the shade spectrum. The camouflage patches covered approximately half the tank and were applied in a hard-edged pattern. This order was actually the formalisation of a practice that had begun in the previous September. From Fgst Nr.280255 a circular plate was bolted over the opening for the deep wading gear on the rear deck. This modification was also to be back fitted by units in the field. As the jack was no longer issued with the Tiger II the brackets on the rear hull plate were dropped from production.

November 1944. An order was issued directing that the hangers and fasteners welded to both sides of the turret during manufacture from July 1944 were to be retrofitted to tanks in the field.

December 1944. An order of 20 December directed that all external surfaces of the Tiger II be painted in a base coat of Olivgrün RAL 6003 with a hard edged camouflage pattern of 8017 and 7028. The order does in fact refer to the base colour as Dunkelgrün although the correct RAL number is given. This is not uncommon in wartime documents and the 31 October 1944 order in fact uses contradictory names for colours within the same paragraph. Component manufacturers had been ordered at the end of November to paint all parts in RAL 6003.

The approval was given to fit armour plates over the air intakes on the rear deck and although this was probably never introduced into production.

Dragon Models Ltd
B1-10/F., 603-609 Castle Peak Rd.
Kong Nam Industrial Building
Tsuen Wan, N. T., Hong Kong.
www.dragon-models.com

Dragon USA
1315 John Reed Ct, City of Industry,
CA 91745, USA
www.dragonmodelsusa.com

Tamiya Inc
Shizuoka City, Japan
www.tamiya.com

Trumpeter
NanLong Industrial Park,SanXiang,
ZhongShan,GuangDong, China
www.trumpeter-china.com

Hobby Boss
NanLong Industrial Park,SanXiang,
ZhongShan,GuangDong, China
www.hobbyboss.com

Academy Plastic Models
521-1, Yonghyeon-dong, Uijeongbu-si,
Gyeonggi-do, Korea
Www.academy.co.kr

Hobby Fan/ AFV Club
6F ., No.183, Sec. 1, Datong Rd, Xizhi City
Taipei County 221, Taiwan
www.hobbyfan.com

Royal Model
Via E. Montale, 19-95030 Pedara, Italy
www.royalmodel.com

Italeri S.p.A.
via Pradazzo 6/b
40012 Calderara di Reno
Bologna, Italy
www.italeri.com

Rye Field Models
www.ryefield-model.com
An almost non-existent web site. I would
recommend one of the on-line retailers.

Hauler
Jan Sobotka
Moravská 38
620 00 Brno
Czech Republic
www.hauler.cz

Voyager
Room 501, No.411 4th Village
SPC Jinshan District
Shanghai 200540
P.R.China
www.voyagermodel.com

Griffon Model
Suite 501, Bldg 01, 418 Middle Longpan
Road, Nanjing, China
www.griffonmodel.com
Since writing this book Griffon have added a
number of Tiger items to their catalogue

Aber
ul. Jalowcowa 15, 40-750 Katowice, Poland
www.aber.net.pl

E.T. Models
www.etmodeller.com

Friulmodel
H 8142. Urhida, Nefelejcs u. 2., Hungary
Www.friulmodel.hu

Modelkasten
Chiyoda-ku Kanda, Nishiki-Cho 1-7, Tokyo,
Japan
www.modelkasten.com
Very difficult to navigate but worthwhile

ROCHM Model
www.rochmmodel.com
rochmmodel@gmail.com

Eduard Model Accessories
Mirova 170, 435 21 Obrnice
Czech Republic
www.eduard.com

Brach Model
Via Candia 23
10010 Barone Canavese, Italy
www.brachmodel.it

Master Box
p.b. 4729,
Dnepropetrovsk
49094, Ukraine
www.mbltd.info

Model Artisan Mori
Yasutsugu Mori
Maison Suiryu 302, Kunoshiro-cho 1-10
Yokkaichi-City, Mie 510-0072, Japan
Www.artisanmori.web.fc2.com

Model Factory Hiro
Yubinbango 121-0063 Adachi-ku, Tokyo
Higashihokima 2-Chome, 3-8 Japan
www.modelfactoryhiro.com

RB Model
Powstancow Wlkp.29B
64-360 Zbaszyn
Poland
Www.rbmodel.com

M Workshop Singapore
91 Bencoolen St Sunshine Plaza01-58
Singapore
Www.themworkshop.com

Zvezda (Zvezda-America)
www.zvezda-usa.com

The purpose of this book is not to definitively document the development, operational history and markings employed by the heavy Panzer units. Rather I have endeavoured to give the general reader an understanding of an enthralling yet complex subject and provide the modeller with the information and inspiration to create a scale representation of these fascinating vehicles. In compiling the unit histories I drew heavily on the works of Oberst Wolfgang Schneider, the autobiographical account of Otto Carious and to a lesser extent the books of Franz Kurowski. I would also recommend Tiger by Egon Kleine and Volkmar Kühn although it is difficult to obtain and has only been published in German. No book on the Tiger tanks could be written without reference to the Germany's Tiger Tanks volumes by the late Thomas L. Jentz and Hilary L. Doyle. Another invaluable resource are Thomas Jentz's Panzertruppen books which I would recommend to any reader with an interest in German armour. I should also acknowledge the contributors to the Axis History and the Feldgrau forums, especially Martin Block and the late Ron Klages whose research on unit histories and vehicle allocations would fill many volumes and Hartmut von Holdt of Tiger in Focus. I would like to thank the modellers who graciously allowed me to publish the images of their work and particularly Bernard Cher, who brought most of them together, and Rupert Harding at Pen & Sword for his advice, assistance and above all patience. Of the product manufacturers I must make special mention of Roberto Reale of Royal Model, Sheng Hui of ROCHM, Jan Zdiarsky from Eduard Accessories and Freddie Leung of Dragon Models who all helped enormously. As always, I am indebted to Karl Berne, Valeri Polokov and J.Howard Parker for their invaluable assistance with the photographs and period insignia.

FURTHER READING

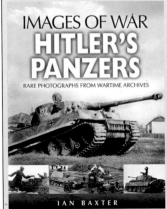
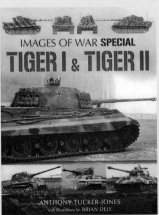
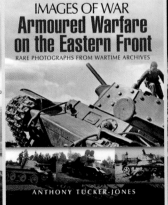